PRAISE FOR
THE BEST YEAR OF OUR LIVES

"*The Best Year of Our Lives* is a timely beacon of hope. Robert Lofthouse, with an affection and passion that comes through in every sentence, recounts a very special year for a very special high school football team in a very special place—small-town America. A town rallies around an underdog team. Players care about each other on and off the field. Coaches help young men develop character traits that will last a lifetime. Lofthouse, with vivid specificity, develops themes that will engage any reader: playing for something greater than yourself; appreciating the power of community; understanding that winning is important but pales in comparison to playing the game—and living life—in a way that is fulfilling and meaningful. Football as a life primer. This book will leave you feeling warm, hopeful, and inspired."

—Alfredo Botello, award-winning author of *180 Days*

"In my thirty-nine years as a sportswriter, I have rarely covered a team that was as much fun as the 2015 Saucon Valley football team. The Panthers enjoyed an epic campaign that saw league and district titles and all kinds of individual success. But more than that, the team was unusually close, a real *Band of Brothers* feeling that Mr. Lofthouse captures perfectly. He's at his best describing one of the best football games I have ever seen, the Panthers' 42–35 back-and-forth donnybrook with Notre Dame. Mr. Lofthouse makes the Panthers come alive, recording their collective passion for the sport and each other with flair and enthusiasm. Any football fan would enjoy this fine read."

—Brad Wilson, senior sportswriter, Lehigh Valley Live

"In over thirty-five years of covering high school, college, and professional teams, the story of the Saucon Valley 2015 football team is one of the few that stand out in my memory for its thrilling victories, unique personalities, and great storylines. Robert Lofthouse was there for it all and gives both die-hard and casual gridiron fans a front-row seat with in-depth insights on everything that transpired during this magical year. With background information on the players, coaches, and school administrators before the season began all the way through to the season's biggest wins, Rob brings you all the great stories and captures the big moments with tremendous details.

"Saucon Valley is a rare community that represents the best of both worlds—a large, vibrant community that still loves, supports, and appreciates its local Friday-night high school football . . . and all that comes with those great traditions. As someone who witnessed and called 'the Catch' on a local TV station, it gave me goosebumps to relive all those magical moments that Rob captured in great details from that historic season."

—Chris Michael, sports director and media services manager, Astound Broadband

"Rob Lofthouse does a masterful job drawing in readers to the point that they become fans of the team, even if they've never stepped foot in the state of Pennsylvania, much less strapped on the shoulder pads for the Panthers."

—David Smale, sportswriter, author of twenty-eight books

"The Saucon Valley football community should be super proud of the light [Lofthouse has] shed on this memorable group of young men, their families, coaches, and others surrounding the program."

—Tom Housenick, senior reporter, *The Morning Call*

"I really enjoyed the book! After finishing it, you feel like you know these players and coaches. The best thing I can say is that I wish every high school athlete could have an experience like these kids did. It just proves that hard work, selflessness, and a sense of pride in each other is still possible in this day and age. Great . . . attention to detail! The book puts you right there in the middle of this great experience!"

—Dan Kendra, assistant coach, Allentown Central Catholic

"Good stuff! It did, in fact, fire up some great memories!"

—Keith Riefenstahl, sportswriter

"Rob Lofthouse will keep you on the edge of your seat, sharing the story of a once-in-a-generation season centered around teamwork, friendship, and community. The season eventually comes to an end while facing a seemingly insurmountable opponent, but not before the memories for a lifetime are formed. Immerse yourself in the story and enjoy this unforgettable season."

—Bob Frey, athletic director (2007–2023), Saucon Valley School District

"Wow! If perspectives are memories of life, then this book is a body of those memories recollected as stories—stories as compelling, as vivid, as vibrant as the thing, the perspective, itself."

—Matthew Evancho, head football coach (2008–2015), Saucon Valley Panthers

The Best Year of our Lives

by Robert E. Lofthouse

© Copyright 2024 Robert E. Lofthouse

ISBN 979-8-88824-575-0

All rights reserved. No part of this publication may be reproduced, stored in a retrieval system, or transmitted in any form or by any means—electronic, mechanical, photocopy, recording, or any other—except for brief quotations in printed reviews, without the prior written permission of the author.

Published by
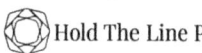 Hold The Line Press LLC

10820 Northridge Drive
Kansas City, KS 66109
www.holdthelinepress.com

THE BEST YEAR
OF
OUR LIVES

ROBERT E. LOFTHOUSE

Hold The Line Press LLC

If you watched the Panthers play on any given weekend, I'm curious to hear about your pregame and postgame traditions. Did you celebrate with friends or family? Maybe you had a lucky pregame meal or postgame dance? Look for *The Best Year of Our Lives* on my website and share your rituals in the comment section on my blog: holdthelinepress.com/the-best-year-of-our-lives.

CONTENTS

FOREWORD 7

PROLOGUE 9

CHAPTER 1: SMALL TOWN AMERICA 12

CHAPTER 2: FOUR HORSEMEN OF THE APOCALYPSE 18

CHAPTER 3: RUN-UP TO 2015 25

CHAPTER 4: DAWNING OF A NEW SEASON 33

CHAPTER 5: TUNE UP GAMES 40

CHAPTER 6: NORTHERN LEHIGH BULLDOGS 48

CHAPTER 7: CATASAUQUA ROUGH RIDERS 53

CHAPTER 8: PEN ARGYL GREEN KNIGHTS 57

CHAPTER 9: WILSON AREA WARRIORS 61

CHAPTER 10: BANGOR SLATERS 64

CHAPTER 11: SALISBURY FALCONS 68

CHAPTER 12: THE BACKYARD BRAWL 72

CHAPTER 13: PAYBACK! 83

CHAPTER 14: COLONIAL LEAGUE GAME OF THE YEAR 92

CHAPTER 15: BICENTENNIAL CUP 109

CHAPTER 16: SEASON-ENDING MUSINGS 112

CHAPTER 17: DISTRICT XI PLAY-OFF GAME ... 118

CHAPTER 18: DISTRICT XI CHAMPIONSHIP ... 130

CHAPTER 19: REGIONAL SEMIS ... 139

CHAPTER 20: CULVER RAN LIKE A MAN TONIGH ... 149

CHAPTER 21: WHO'S TEP? ... 160

CHAPTER 22: BEYOND 2015 ... 179

CHAPTER 23: LEGACY ... 189

EPILOGUE ... 204

ACKNOWLEDGMENTS ... 210

REFERENCES ... 215

APPENDIX A: TEAM PHOTO ... 216

APPENDIX B: DAY IN THE LIFE OF A FOOTBALL PROGRAM ... 217

APPENDIX C: PIAA, DISTRICT XI & COLONIAL LEAGUE ... 220

APPENDIX D: PHOTO GALLERY ... 223

*To you, the reader of this book,
thank you for embarking on this thrilling journey with me.*

FOREWORD

THE 2015 SEASON was magical for the Saucon Valley High School football team. To the outside world, the Panthers came from out of nowhere to advance to the Pennsylvania Class AAA state championship semifinal game. That wasn't true, which is one of the reasons this is such a special story.

I jumped on the bandwagon after it had already gathered momentum, and I rode it to the end. What sticks in my mind as I look back almost a decade later is how this team grew together. They exceeded most experts' expectations because they all got along so well—on and off the field. Most of the players on the team grew up together. They played other sports together and developed a chemistry that is rare for a high school team.

Successful high school football teams who have the support of their communities are not always made up of best friends. But this team was. The result of that closeness was that they didn't have a lot of close games, and that wasn't always because they were the more talented team. They just had a way of playing together, with each other and for each other.

The first time they demonstrated their resilience came in Week Eight, when they faced another unbeaten team, Notre Dame-Green Pond. The Panthers jumped out to a big lead, but Notre Dame-Green Pond made a dramatic comeback to tie the game with about one minute left on the clock. That team had no business coming back, but after they did, it would have been easy for Saucon Valley to fold. That's when the Panthers really showed what they were made of.

Good team chemistry shows when the players don't care who

the hero is. That was true all season for Saucon Valley, but it was especially true in that game. While the Panthers had a great group of seniors, it was a sophomore outside of that core group of guys who made the game-winning catch—known locally as *The Catch!* Other players were thrilled to see this sophomore make the biggest play of his life to win the game of the year.

I covered many of their games, especially that Notre Dame game. But Rob Lofthouse got to see every game. When you're writing about a team, whether it's a professional sports team or a high school team, to tell the whole story you have to be there and be familiar with the players and the audience. With the Saucon Valley 2015 football team, Rob was that guy.

Rob knew who hung out with whom and where they went when they hung out. That's something that only someone who has a true knowledge of the subject can portray. You can't fake that.

Few could tell this story better than Rob, who watched and recorded every win, every challenge and every shared moment that cemented this team as legendary. Join him as he revisits this unforgettable season—a season filled with the roar of the crowd, the grit on the players' faces, and the unyielding spirit of a small town united. This is a testament to the power of teamwork, small-town spirit and memories that will be cherished by players, coaches, and fans for years to come.

—Tom Housenick, senior reporter, *The Morning Call*, Allentown, Pennsylvania

PROLOGUE

MUD-STAINED KNEES AND grass-streaked smiles—that's what marked the beginning of their bond. Back then, they were scrawny eight-year-olds, tackling each other on the youth football field. Each hit, each fumble recovered, built a brick in the foundation of their self-confidence. Skills grew alongside their height, their laughter echoing through afternoons spent under the relentless summer sun. These weren't just teammates; they were a chosen family. On the field, they pushed each other to their limits, a silent vow to never let their brother fall. Off the field, that loyalty remained. They were there for scraped elbows and broken hearts, celebrating victories big and small. High school brought diversification. Wrestling mats, basketball courts, and baseball diamonds beckoned to some. Yet, through it all, football remained a constant, a shared language that transcended the boundaries of other sports. Now, years later, Thanksgiving isn't just about turkey and stuffing. It's a reunion, a pilgrimage back to the field where they became men. The worn grass beneath their cleats is a testament to their enduring bond, a promise whispered on the autumn breeze: these pickup games, these shared memories, will continue as long as they can stand.

Every Friday night as high schoolers, the Panthers weren't just playing for a win; they were playing for something bigger. Coach Matt Evancho built a program that went beyond touchdowns and tackles. Here, under the Friday night lights, character was the ultimate victory. Over countless practices and game days, Evancho instilled in his players not just physical toughness, but also mental fortitude, camaraderie, and leadership. They were a band of brothers, learning life lessons that would extend far beyond the football field.

The following, just one of their many stories, leads off this retrospective, and captures the innocence of their youth.

Fridays were electric. Everyone decked out in jerseys, school spirit roared through the air. Cheerleaders and band members wore their uniforms. The whole school buzzed with anticipation for the game of the week. It was a day unlike any other.

Pregame

The boys had their pregame and postgame rituals. Nate Harka, Kory Kemmerer, and their buddies had a standing tradition. Right after school, they would head straight to Kory's house. His parents, absolute champs, had a buffalo chicken pizza waiting for them—the legendary kind from Roma, a local favorite. Buffalo chicken pizza might not have been the most performance-enhancing pregame meal (looking at you, Hogs!), but for them, it was the perfect way to kick off game day.

They'd hang out, goof around, and enjoy each other's company. That core group of guys were family throughout high school.

Fueled by their friendship and pizza, they'd pile into a single car overflowing with teenage enthusiasm. Destination: the field house. It was the spot to meet up with the team before the game, energy of the moment sizzled as they prepped for battle.

Postgame

Victory waffles! Following the after-game celebrations, there were two popular destinations: the locker room showers (eventually) and the Waffle House. The Waffle House, on Main Street in Hellertown, was a special place for postgame rituals. Especially after beating Southern Lehigh. Nate Harka adds, "We also had our own hangout spots. My house, with its basement, was a popular choice. But sometimes we'd head to Goodie's place for a bonfire out back in his giant field. The linemen would bring their trucks, tailgates open, enjoying good company and food."

Every year, these players relentlessly pushed each other to surpass their previous bests, setting new standards.

We all had our postgame rituals. Mine started with a jolt of predawn enthusiasm, fueled by echoes of the previous night's game. The scoreboard had gone dark, but the thrill of victory lingered. As the first rays of sunlight peeked through the trees on Saturday morning, I'd grab a cup of coffee and finish up my stats from the night before, recording the new career statistical leaders, reviewing the local sports stories, I'd scour the league standings to see who else had won. Then I'd head out to tackle my sprawling acre and a half of lawn. The rhythmic whir of the mower somehow helped me process the game, replaying key moments in my head. Every stripe I cut in the grass felt symbolic, a fresh start after the emotional roller coaster of a game the night before.

Growing Up on the Gridiron
Nate Harka shares more fond memories, "Most of us were together the whole way through. I'd say probably ninety percent of the guys on the team came up through the ranks together—the whole Saucon Valley Youth Football Association. It was like a family. We knew each other since flag football days, way back when we were just learning the ropes of tackle football."

The cool thing about being from a small town is the chance to play sports together with your buddies your whole life, from elementary school right up to graduation. The best part? Familiar faces. These weren't just teammates; they were friends, some practically brothers, who'd been playing together since they were kids. This shared history, forged in countless practices, victories, and defeats, had fostered a camaraderie that was as powerful as any play on the field. It was a bond that fueled their determination and made them more than just the sum of their parts.

CHAPTER 1

SMALL TOWN AMERICA

We were just a young team, trying to figure it out. We knew we were talented, but were very underdeveloped.
—Evan Culver, Saucon Valley Panther (2012–2015)

WHY THIS BOOK? WHY NOW?

Christian Carvis's freshman season was a rough one. His coach moved the five-foot-seven, one hundred fifty pounder from defensive line to linebacker, but it didn't go well at first. "I hated it," this 2015 cocaptain recalled. "I begged and pleaded to go back to the defensive line."

Senior classmate and cocaptain Mike Kane didn't have a blast that year, either. "I started on defense, and we were in a lot of games," Kane recalled, "but we ended up four and seven, letting a lot of games slip through our fingers."

After that dismal record, these two players became key contributors in a remarkable turnaround season in 2013. Carrying that momentum into 2014, they clawed their way to a share of the Colonial League Championship and a coveted berth in the District XI Class AAA final. But the final game was a heartbreaker. Facing a seemingly unstoppable and dominant Bethlehem Catholic team, they fell in a lopsided defeat. The disappointment was palpable, but it couldn't diminish the incredible journey they were taking.

Evan Culver, cocaptain and the team's star running back, spent that following summer of 2015 with his dad in Seattle. Focused on improving his game, he sensed a lot of the guys were doing the same thing. "That 2014 season-ending game was a real turning point for us." Culver said. "We were just a young team trying to figure it out." Shaking his head slightly, he went on, "We knew we were talented, but were very underdeveloped. We hadn't fully grown into ourselves as individuals or as a team. So that Bethlehem Catholic game exposed our weaknesses. We were hungry to win it, but that defeat left a bitter taste in our mouths. You know what? That game was a wake-up call. We learned some tough lessons in that game and became a stronger team in the long run. We had a chip on our shoulder, you know. We wanted to win and weren't satisfied losing that playoff game."

Lower Saucon Township and Hellertown Pennsylvania are small-town America. These are the towns making up a working-class high school district that loves football and slowly, steadily, over the course of eleven years, built a powerhouse of a skilled team that won back-to-back-to-back championships, going on to compete at the highest level ever in the history of the Saucon Valley School District.

The 2015 Pennsylvania Interscholastic Athletic Association (PIAA) football season will become the theatre of operations for what this book is about.

So in answering the opening questions, let's walk back through a brief background to see how the stage was set for their moment in history.

A gridiron team from Saucon Valley had never played after Thanksgiving. Their trophy case held a couple of dusty league championship relics from bygone eras. Most seasons ended with a thud; mediocre records were a familiar refrain for over forty years. But this year, something felt different. The whispers started in the locker room, a quiet belief that this year could be different. Maybe it was the unyielding determination in the eyes of their captains. Perhaps it was the innovative schemes cooked up by their coaching staff. Whatever the reason, a contagious confidence pulsed through the team.

What went on behind the scenes? How would this year be different?

"There might be a family connection," Zach Thatcher, the star quarterback and cocaptain, mused. "A lot of our parents and grandparents went to either Saucon Valley or Hellertown High. But maybe it's simpler than that. We all just started playing football together when we were kids and that bond stuck."

Saucon Valley plays sports in a Colonial League made up of small schools in the Lehigh Valley of east central Pennsylvania. In a big way that goes to the heart of what small town America is all about—close-knit communities. This football team would win over the hearts and minds of Hellertown and Lower Saucon Township. Through those friendships and attention, they drew in fans from outside the enclave of the Lehigh Valley.

Vickie Wolfe, a dedicated team mom, describes the emotional bond that sustained the fanbase during those 2012–2015 seasons. "Our community truly came together like a family," she said, her voice filled with warmth. "We felt incredibly fortunate to be part of this team, and the friendships we formed back then are as strong as ever."

One of the defining characteristics of small towns is the strong sense of community. People often know each other well, look out for each other, having a shared sense of local history and identity. They live life together, some worship together, some play sports, do backyard barbeques together, sit around the bonfires swapping stories. Some vacation together, many work in their hometown, and some commute to far-away cities like Morristown, Philadelphia, or New York. Neighbors gather in the same community for years and even if the kids leave for a time to find their career and start their own families, they often return to their roots. The veins of this community run deep in the lives of many I interviewed for this book. As I said, families trace their roots back generations with their histories intertwined. Their parents were well-acquainted, and grandparents even more so. Some would leave to move on with their lives. New arrivals may or may not fit in, depending on their interpersonal dynamics and what skills they brought to the field. On Fridays in the fall, the heritage comes alive. Dads and grandfathers, former players on Saucon Valley or Hellertown High football teams, root for the next generation. The moms and grandmothers, former players, and teenage fans all echo their cheers from the stands. Some formerly played musical instruments in the marching band, twirled batons, carried banners. The gameday announcer, a constant voice for over a quarter-century at the middle school, JV, and varsity levels, embodies this enduring spirit. Many of the high schools in the Colonial League can make similar claims.

From my perspective as a parent and fan, it was the best five-dollar-entertainment in the valley. During football season, it was the community's way. That's what you do on Friday night. You go down to watch your football team, win or lose.

The Backstory
In the 2013 season, the team's success created a murmur of hope for their prospects of a great ending. The roar of the crowd echoed throughout Montford Illick Stadium as the Panthers intercepted another pass in the endzone. It was a scene I witnessed countless times over eight seasons. While recording stats alongside my wife and daughter in the press box for about 170 varsity and junior varsity (JV) games, we saw the fumbles, missed opportunities, and frustrating losses too! From scorching August sunshine to snow-covered fields, rain delays, the mud games, thrilling victories, agonizing defeats, and injuries on the field, we experienced it all—JV and varsity.

Alongside our dear friend, gameday announcer Gail Nolf, the dedicated scorekeepers, reporters, and Panther fans, we discovered the magic that drew people from hundreds of miles around. It wasn't just about the game; community spirit was thriving.

Through interviews with coaches, players, parents, and friends,

I delved deeper into the heart of this community. What I found was a place where values mattered and camaraderie bloomed, with these friendships forming an unshakeable bond. Remember the electricity in the air on those autumn Friday nights? The roar of the crowd as the Panthers took the field, the shared hope and anticipation that painted the stands Saucon Valley red and black? In this book, we revisit those legendary moments, relive the triumphs and tribulations of your beloved Saucon Valley Panthers. Rediscover the magic that made them more than just a team—we were a family, a community, a legacy that continues to inspire.

Bob Frey and I collaborated on this book along with players, coaches, parents, sports reporters, and dedicated fans who all made the season unforgettable. This book, *The Best Year of Our Lives*, will keep the legacy of this team alive for generations to come. We hope their story of character, leadership, honor, and respect for one another inspires others to achieve their own greatness.

In fact, let me focus on one more quote from Carvis, longtime member of the Hogs. "The Hogs" was a term of endearment to the Panther linemen who played their hearts out. Offensively, their blocking pushed opposing defenders down the field, opening holes for their ball carriers to make big gains. Defensively, these Hogs attacked with a Marine-like discipline to plug holes and prevent opposing ball carriers from gaining much ground. Coach Chromczak will say these linemen made their team success possible.

The Hogs, Photo credit: Keith Riefenstahl, *Saucon Source*

Christian was one of the leaders of this team from 2012 to 2015, calling defensive plays from his linebacker position.

"The Saucon community is important to me because it was in my blood through and through. This group of guys grew up playing and loving the game together. From eighty-pound football leading all the way up to our senior year we fought together year after year and created bonds that are still strong today. We had a fair amount of success when we were younger, enjoyed being around each other, and that was ultimately what mattered the most. Some of my best friends, and likely best men at my wedding one day, have come from this team. The times we shared together on the field are memorable and priceless. With that being said the community not only had our back, but they also lived through us in a way. Hellertown has a tremendous amount of character as a town. In a way we embodied that as a team. We were not the biggest, strongest, or most talented team, but we had character, heart, and most of all, each other. That, in a way, is a metaphor for Hellertown."

Small-town America, in plain view.

CHAPTER 2

FOUR HORSEMEN OF THE APOCALYPSE

It was a fun atmosphere.
—Phil Sams, Saucon Valley receivers coach

A WELL-FUNCTIONING FOOTBALL team thrives on leadership, both on the sidelines and on the field. While the coaches provide strategic guidance, the heart and soul of on-field leadership resides with this exceptional group of seniors—my "Captains Courageous."

You'll encounter them throughout this story, but their impact extends far beyond what they did in high school. Each year, Coach Evancho initiates a vital tradition: the players are invited to elect who they want to lead them as captains. The coaching staff does not participate in these elections. Remarkably, these player-chosen leaders consistently align with the coaches' own private assessments.

For the 2015 season, Christian Carvis (middle linebacker and offensive guard), Michael Kane (tight end and defensive end), Zach Thatcher (quarterback and free safety), and Evan Culver (running back and corner back) emerged as the players' choices, earning the respected title of cocaptains.

Cocaptains Michael Kane, Zach Thatcher, Christian Carvis, Evan Culver. Photo credit: Keith Riefenstahl, *Saucon Source*

Do You Feel the Energy?

There was always a buzz in the air on game day. Were you decked out in black and red, a sea of Panther pride swaying in unison? Maybe you were part of the legendary Jungle, cheers echoing through the stadium. Did the booming sounds of the "Tuba Hump" get you in the mood for ground pounding football? That's what we called it, a catchy little tune to get people moving to the beat of the band and ready for the game. Perhaps your house was a beacon of team spirit, adorned with red and black bows, signs and banners. Did you travel hundreds of miles to away games, or were you a regular at the home field? Were you part of the pregame energy, helping set the stage for victory? Did you work tirelessly in the press box, on the sidelines, or even serve up hot dogs, hot coffee, or hot chocolate in the concession stands?

How about Thursday evening team meals in the school cafeteria? Are you a mom who prepared the Thanksgiving Day breakfast for the boys as they prepared for a playoff game scheduled to follow the next day, Black Friday? Did you go shopping or attend the game or do both?

Coach, play, or watch, did you suit up to do your part supporting the Panthers on the field? Is Coach Evancho still wearing shorts in December? Who gave players free haircuts? What about the postgame celebrations?

Did you line the sidewalks, cheer them on as they left home for their next challenge and then late at night welcome back the weary warriors, returning from another slugfest somewhere in eastern Pennsylvania?

Who rode the fan bus?

This book isn't just for the players and coaches who led the team to glory. It's a call to all Saucon Valley alumni, family, and friends to relive these unforgettable moments and recapture the magic of those glory days.

In a broader sense we tell the story of how this small town came together to support an amazing team and rode the rocket fueling and propelling them to the PIAA final four.

Not Saucon! A final four appearance had never been done before.

While watching the team during a 2009 preseason scrimmage in Exton, I recall hearing the opposing team's fans remarking that Saucon was always easy pickings, good for a win. The football winning tradition was just not a constant for the Panthers in those years.

It took a long time. It took hard work. A little luck? Yeah, but coaches led the way and then got out of the way to let their thoroughbreds do what they did best: play winning football!

Coaches taught football techniques and helped to grow young boys into young men.

Players put in the hard work, sweating through the July and August practices.

Family and friends watched, cheered, and hoped for better outcomes.

We all became believers.

This Saucon team wasn't just about wins and losses. There was an undeniable magic in their manner, a special energy that propelled them to a remarkable nineteen victories in two years. Their predecessors, despite valiant efforts, could only manage a fraction of that success in the previous six seasons. What made these guys so different? There was a certain je ne sais quoi, a special aura that surrounded them.

From the beginning, they went about their business with a focused purpose in mind.

Their audacious goals for the 2015 season were etched in stone:
- Conquer the Colonial League and win the title
- Vanquish BECA (Bethlehem Catholic)
- Claim the District XI AAA Championship

For the Saucon Valley Panthers, this trifecta wasn't just wishful thinking; it was a relentless pursuit fueled by recent years of narrowly missing these very milestones. This season, they were determined to rewrite history. Achieving all three goals would be a monumental feat, a testament to their unwavering dedication and a story forever etched in Saucon Valley football lore. (For those unfamiliar, the Colonial League is a local conference with twelve teams, and the District XI AAA Championship is a regional title, which some forty teams target.)

Youth Football

Winning wasn't new to them; it had been ingrained in their DNA since youth football. Self-assurance, genuine and unwavering, marked their every step.

Take Coach Brown for example. Coach Brown is a legend around here. He's still coaching the 125-pound team today exactly the same way he coached back then. Harka adds, "Our team was like a family—a lot of dads took turns coaching, including mine. Guys like Gino and Eric Schneider were all there from the flag football days, all the way up to the 125-pound league. By fifth grade things changed. We transitioned to middle school with a new coaching staff and a different approach. Back then, making it to the 125-pound team was a major accomplishment. It felt like you'd almost graduated to high school football! We were at the top of the youth football pyramid, and it was a big deal!"

Building Endurance: Flag Football to Full Pads
Talk about dedication! Back in the day, some would play a flag football game then immediately suit up in full pads for another game. That's the kind of football-focused guys they were, pushing to the limit, enjoying the game.

Taught by their legendary coach, Matt Evancho, these players embodied a philosophy that transcended the game: "Respect each other, learn to love each other, and come together as champions. Have fun and enjoy it all." Coach Evancho wasn't just a coach; he was a constant source of inspiration, reminding his players of this mantra every week and after every game, year after year.

Embarking on a quest for their second consecutive shot at a league title in the fall of 2015, the greatest senior class in school history took the field during the heat of August with, I say somewhat cynically, every football player's favorite: two-a-day practices in the summer heat!

Panther Varsity History
We had seen other Colonial League teams come to town in prior years and mop up the field with our Panthers. We watched as squads from the Wilson Warriors, Catasauqua Rough Riders, Bangor Slaters, Pen Argyl Green Knights, Northern Lehigh Bulldogs, Northwestern Lehigh Tigers, and Southern Lehigh Spartans all took turns thrashing the boys from Hellertown—hanging sixty points on

us one week and shutting us out another week.

The Colonial League had a familiar pattern: Saucon Valley often found itself battling Notre Dame-Green Pond, Salisbury, Palmerton, and a revolving door of other teams for a mid-to-lower-league finish. Wilson was on top but in 2007 Evancho took the helm at Saucon Valley, aiming to build his own program. A few years later, Bret Comp, Wilson's longtime head coach, departed for Parkland, where he helped to coach a AAAA team to the state championship game. Wilson, once boasting championship trophies and recent memories of their PIAA championship run as a perennial league leader, found themselves sinking to the bottom of the league alongside the others. A new era had begun in the Colonial League, with the balance of power moving around the league.

In 2013 Saucon Valley rediscovered winning as this Panther squad stormed into high school. We saw our athletes put the pieces of a championship run together. We won the Eastern Conference Tournament in 2013. We earned league cochamp honors with Southern Lehigh and Northwestern Lehigh in 2014, playing in the District XI AAA championship game before losing in embarrassment to (BECA) Bethlehem Catholic. We were in the press box with some of the sports reporters from throughout the Valley, listening to some of the chatter before and during the game. Based on the team's history, most didn't give Saucon Valley a chance against BECA. But it was fun to watch from that vantage point high up in the sky of one of the more fabled high school stadiums in eastern Pennsylvania.

The 2014 Panther Hogs returned in 2015 as the local version of the horsemen of the apocalypse, a reference to the Book of Revelation in the New Testament of the Bible. Each horseman represents a different aspect of the apocalypse. In the biblical account, the first horseman symbolizes conquest or victory, the second represents great conflict, the third represents hardship, and the fourth, well, he just unleashes hell. Our Hog horsemen heralded a period of cataclysmic events about to come upon their opponents. I'll leave it to you to visualize which player on this team represented which horseman at any given point in time throughout this season.

The whole line had come back—Cody Zrinski, Trey Polack, Ryan Meyers, Stephen Good, Christian Carvis, and Mike Kane. With record-setters Thatcher, Culver, Kane, Harka, Carvis, and Mike Paolini strapping on their pads, everybody went to work. School-season and career records, some nursing cobwebs for twenty-plus years, began to fall under their skill. New standards were about to be set.

Looking around the league at our competition, this was the year Southern Lehigh Spartans quarterback, Blake Levengood, would throw for a school-record 2,417 yards. He also tied Travis Edmond's record for TD passes in a season with twenty-four. We would have to shut him down. Teammate Ethan Price posted a school-record twenty-one career TD catches for 1,874 yards lifetime. We would have to contain him. Salisbury's Tevon Weber threw for twenty-four TD passes this season, giving him a program-record forty-nine for his career. He's the first quarterback we faced in the regular season. He'd nearly beat us the previous year. Northwestern's Harry Hall finished out his career with a total of fifty-seven career TDs, six more than the previous school record. He had beaten us the previous year. All were formidable performances the Panthers could only watch with awe in previous years. But this year, the Panthers arrived at the head of the class and would game plan for each challenge.

Glory days!

CHAPTER 3

RUN-UP TO 2015

You're about to hear the rest of the story.
—Paul Harvey

HEAD COACH DICK BOWMAN took the Panthers to the District XI playoffs in 2004, after winning the school's second league title in nearly fifty years.

Following the 2006 season, Coach Bowman retired, and athletic director Bob Frey made a strategic move setting his sights on Matt Evancho, who was then defensive coordinator at Wilson Area High School. Frey needed someone to reignite Saucon Valley's winning spirit after a lackluster 2–8 season. Evancho's credentials were impressive. As Wilson's defensive mastermind, he'd played a crucial role in their 2006 Colonial League Championship run alongside head coach Bret Comp. Evancho's defensive prowess, coupled with his experience in building championship teams, made him the perfect candidate to lead Saucon Valley back.

He had prepped just down the road at Easton High, a perennial powerhouse ranked among the top ten winningest high school football programs of all time. Today they boast an incredible win-loss record of 822–344–52, a testament to their ability to develop talented athletes year after year. Evancho's playing career continued at Penn State under legendary coach Joe Paterno, where he honed his skills as a linebacker for a program that consistently ranked in the nation's top twenty-five of Division I football teams. This championship experience wasn't limited to playing. He understood what it took to win, and he planned to revive that culture at Saucon Valley. After all, throughout his career, he'd only been associated with winning football. This hire inspired confidence in the future of the organization.

The dream began for Coach Evancho and Saucon Valley as a quick reality check. Six seasons passed, each one a tide pulling them back and forth in the standings. Losing records in four of those years and sparks of success in the other two—it wasn't the championship picture anyone had envisioned. At its lowest, the varsity football program won only three games in multiple seasons under their new head coach. With a fleeting whisp of success, the '07 and '08 teams posted a better than .500 record, and that was it. They didn't get back in the plus column again until 2013. That team played their way into the Pennsylvania Eastern Conference Tournament—winning it all and posting a 9–3 final record, the best since the '04 team had won their title, their first championship in nine years. Finally, they were heading in the right direction.

A seemingly ordinary series of events occurring at the end of the 2012 season served as a potent omen, compelling Matt to make a vital decision that would shape his legacy. This emotional nudge made him acutely aware of the preciousness of what he had built.

He was always known for his intensity. He held fast to his coaching philosophy, emphasizing discipline and execution. Getting players and coaches to fully embrace his vision was key. He instilled a relentless work ethic and winning mentality, brick by brick. The coaching staff bought in. The players bought in, and something exciting was taking hold. Football became fun in Saucon Valley again—for players and fans alike.

Imagine a high-powered offense, suffocating defense, and a team hungry to prove itself. This, combined with the arrival of a truly exceptional transfer student, Evan Culver, created a perfect storm. Like a master sailor harnessing a raging sea, by the fall of 2013, Evancho had finally navigated the power and size of the

Colonial League, bringing the thrill of victory back to Saucon Valley.

After missing the 2013 district playoffs with a 7–3 Colonial League record, the Panthers went north to play in a consolation tournament—a two-game winner-takes-all contest on successive weekends. The Panthers beat Jim Thorpe High School by two scores behind the steady quarterbacking arm of senior Keith Mosher, the punishing ground game of senior Nick Savant, and the Hogs, who were just getting started. Culver watched and learned from his "savant" as the backup tailback in their now famous I-formation. Thatcher was the free safety on that team and played backup quarterback to Mosher.

The Rise of the Hogs and Savant's Legacy
Saucon Valley built a reputation for defensive prowess, known for shutting down opponents "between the sticks." Behind this stalwart defense, a new offensive force was emerging—an early iteration of the Hogs that would become legendary.

It wasn't lost on anyone—the players and coaches, the ever-supportive parents, and fans all felt it. Whispers started in the Colonial League, reaching the Lehigh Valley sports media. District XI outside the Colonial League would soon witness it firsthand. Playoff teams would be the next to discover this truth, the hard way.

Leading the charge was Savant, a talented running back who rewrote school record books. He racked up multiple rushing and scoring records, carrying the team on his impressive legs as far as his individual talent could take them. The Hogs, many of whom were sophomores and freshmen on that 2013 team, opened holes in the line for him.

A Nail-Biter in Wilkes-Barre
The following weekend, our Panthers faced a stiffer test further north in Wilkes-Barre, taking on perennial playoff contender James Coughlin High School. Win or lose, this would be the last game of

the year. In a classic ground-and-pound battle that nearly hit the century mark in points, Saucon Valley emerged victorious with a heart-stopping finish. Wonder who made that play?

Each team missed a point after touchdown (PAT) in the first half, then matched each other in the second half. Saucon Valley made a field goal and Coughlin converted two 2-point attempts to knot the score at 43 apiece as time ran out in regulation play. The game came down to the wire, with Coughlin scoring in the last twenty seconds of regulation for the tie. Overtime heroics were needed this time. The overtime period saw the Panther juggernaut score and convert their PAT to go up 50–43. James Coughlin came right back and scored their final touchdown of the evening, tying the score. But rather than kick the extra point for a tie, they went for the win on a pass play. From his cornerback position, Culver rose above the defenders, snatching the game-winning pass out of the air! The crowd erupted in a deafening roar as Culver clutched the ball to his chest. The potent Panther offense, powered by the relentless blocking of the Hogs, had refused to be denied all night. Their leader, senior Savant, workhorse of the team all year, had pounded his way into the end zone five times that night. This incredible performance marked a fitting handoff from the graduating record-setter, Savant, to his successor, the next record-setter in the making, Evan Culver.

Saucon Valley had posted the first nine-win season since Matt Evancho took over the program. Had he finally done it? Had he developed players to fit his game plans and nailed down a winning formula?

With some key players graduating and a career-ending injury to a promising young linebacker, prospects for the next year looked challenging.

The Importance of Depth

Players moving out of the district or playing for private schools highlighted the need for depth. A strong program had developed capable backups to avoid a single injury derailing the entire season. Injuries can disrupt plans, requiring players to step up into unforeseen roles. For example, Nate Kehs stepped into a starting outside linebacker role due to the career-ending injury of the guy positionally ahead of him.

Get ready for the reload
Gifted running backs moving up from the second squad, a promising young quarterback with varsity experience in the secondary, a maturing set of linemen affectionately called the Hogs, and linebackers hungry for action gave Head Coach Evancho a fresh outlook on the future.

Something was different with these Panthers. They picked each other up, encouraged each other on and off the field, laid it all on the line, never took a play off. These guys played with guts, grit, and determination. They were all heart and soul, very workmanlike and rarely got emotional. Other teams would try to get inside their heads and disturb the plan, but Evancho's team kept their focus. This was a different kind of football team than the locals had been accustomed to watching. They bought in. The coaching staff was on board.

So what happened in 2014?

Optimism was in the air. Everything seemed to gel with this squad. Evancho brought back his offensive and defensive starters, many of them in the old high school tradition playing both offense and defense. While losing only one league game to the always dominant Northwestern Lehigh Tigers, Saucon Valley beat archrival Southern Lehigh and Southern Lehigh beat Northwestern to lock up a three-way first-place tie between those three teams. Each of them lost only one game to end the regular season.

Due to school enrollment size, Northwestern played their postseason in AA but the other two were classified as AAA schools. Southern Lehigh and Saucon Valley went on to face each other for the second time in 2014, but for the first time ever in the District XI AAA Playoffs.

Seeded two and three respectively, the Spartans from Southern Lehigh met Saucon Valley with bragging rights in their own "backyard brawl" and a chance to play in the title game. This would prove to be a classic contest.

Saucon faced down their Colonial League archenemy in a meeting that rarely went well for the Panthers. This rivalry customarily turned into hard-fought games with Southern Lehigh winning. True to form, it was a slugfest, but the result was decided by a Giacomo Pazzaglia (Saucon Valley kicker) field goal for a final score of 20–17. Saucon Valley had put up its first ten-win season in ten years by outlasting their Southern Lehigh rivals.

The next game up would be with the Bethlehem Catholic (BECA) Hawks, who'd beaten the Lehighton Indians 48–18 in the other play-off contest.

For only the second time in school history, the Panthers had earned a spot in the District XI Championship Game. Sporting ten-win seasons, the Panthers and Hawks were both pumped up for this title game!

The larger, swifter, more talented BECA team left no doubt who would win this game. Playing with multiple Division I college prospects, they overpowered our boys from the very beginning and won by a large margin of five touchdowns. Thus ended the Panther season in embarrassing fashion—an ugly loss.

While that year's Panthers weren't quite ready, the experience fueled their competitive spirit. They would not let this setback define them. As Culver, now a thousand-yard rusher and record setter in his own right, later said, that team went into the following season with a chip on its shoulder.

Plenty of Football Yet to Play!

As we began deep-diving into the idea of writing *The Best Year of*

Our Lives, Bob Frey said of the 2015 season, "There was no doubt that everyone had their eye on Saucon Valley as a team expected to do well. The biggest challenge for the players was staying focused and taking one game at a time. This was a tall task for the coaching staff but successfully accomplished. Our group of coaches set tough expectations, high standards, and expected hard work from their players, but also produced positive and strong relationships with those players. Those relationships were reciprocal. The coaches believed in the players and the players believed in the coaches. When both entities are on the same page, all the pieces needed for a successful season on and off the field come together. Highs and lows are part of any season in any sport, and we'll see many of them in this story. How you handle the lows determines how successful your team becomes. Our team and coaches learned from their mistakes, gave constructive feedback to each other, picked each other up when seeing a fellow teammate down low, and always thought positively. There was never a sense of defeat or 'we can't do this'. We had a plan for victory."

The heartbeat of Saucon Valley football pulsed through various eating establishments on Main Street. The worn leather of the booths held more than just weary players. It cradled a family. Laughter erupted like popcorn kernels, chasing away the tension of grueling practices. Stories, spun between bites of juicy burgers, solidified camaraderie that transcended the game. Here, parents and coaches weren't just spectators and leaders; they were confidantes and friends. The air buzzed with the comforting hum of conversation, punctuated by the clink of glasses raised in toasts. These weren't just gatherings fueled by burgers and brews, they were threads, invisible yet strong, weaving a tapestry of community that no opponent could tear apart. Despite the success of the 2013 and 2014 seasons, Saucon Valley had flashed a middling .510 record over the previous ten years. Some casual observers were frustrated. Some parents made their emotions known, wanting their kids to have more playing time. But the faithful remained committed. The athletic director felt Coach Evancho's personality, character and leadership outstripped the record. Bob Frey added, "You could see it all coming together because he was teaching the right things. There was never a doubt in my mind about Matt as a head coach. That was proven daily."

Principles taught by Evancho kept the team primed and ready throughout the season.
1. Keep your head on straight, don't do anything dumb.
2. Coaching staff will prepare the kids before each game and give them the tools they need for success.
3. Injuries can be avoided by solid preparation and the kids going all in 100 percent.
4. Some players will gain experience by playing different positions, gaining confidence as the season progresses.
5. Facing Notre Dame later in the 2015 season will give the team time to figure things out, correct their mistakes, and prepare for the most challenging showdown in league play.

Three things Bob Frey always demanded of a coach:
1. Have fun.
2. Develop each athlete better than they were on the first day of the season.
3. Build positive relationships with your athletes.

Coach Evancho led the way and did all three of these daily, every year. His players would run through a wall for him if he asked. They had fun. They worked hard. Those relationships built in many cases are long lasting beyond high school. Many of the players are still in touch, attending each other's weddings and plying their success today with those lessons learned so many years ago.

So how did the 2015 season play out?

CHAPTER 4

DAWNING OF A NEW SEASON

They sent me out to try to tackle Christian, and it didn't quite work. I hit that six-foot one boy and I went backwards on the ground. It was a fun day getting out there, trying to do some of the stuff that the kids do.
—Brenda Carvis, mother of Christian Carvis

CHRIS LABATCH PLAYED high school ball at Wilson in 2006. They won the state AA title. Matt Evancho was his defensive coordinator. They became good friends. Chris was now Matt's defensive coordinator on the Saucon Valley team. Labatch commented on the similarities between the two teams, not so much in the way they played but the closeness in the locker room between the players. "When everyone you know comes out and says we're a family, we care about each other, you saw something special develop with this group of older players helping the younger players. Some of the older players would invite the younger guys out. They actually cared about each other. They weren't just teammates. They truly cared about one another and wanted each other to be successful.

Encouraged by the close calls in 2013 and 2014, the Saucon Valley faithful anticipated a breakthrough season in 2015. Frey offered further insight, explaining, "You could see the growth taking place, the change in the attitude and work ethic of the players, not just with the seniors but down the line. You knew that each year was getting better. The coaching staff believed in each other and in the players coming up through the system. The players believed in a system that was now proven, working, and showing significant progress."

August. Two-A-Days. Brutal Heat and Humidity.
It was a grueling gauntlet by design. Not just required by the coaches—the players craved this intensity. They had unfinished business. A new season dawned, and with it, a fresh resolve.

One practice was held every morning and one every afternoon or evening. When practice was in the evening, they'd hang out at somebody's house, then do it all over again the next day. Sleep, eat, workout, practice football, hang out together, repeat. The players I spoke with said it wasn't like a job—they were laser focused on the mission and having fun together!

The *Easton Express-Times* 2015 Football Preview on LeghighValleyLive.com, released an article from longtime Sports Journalist Brad Wilson.

> Sometimes the best way to evaluate a football team's prospects for the upcoming season starts with assessing its weaknesses. So, first up, Saucon Valley. Well, err, umm, ah . . . (sound of rummaging through notes) there has to be something . . . ah, the Panthers have an inexperienced kicker! There's one. And . . . that's about it.

That kicker was Josh Snead, who as a junior in 2014, had been recruited from the soccer squad. Josh would go on to smash the school's scoring records for kickers, relying largely on kicking single points after touchdowns—one point at a time. Josh played two seasons with a career and school record high of 125 points. I remember thinking that when Josh stepped up to kick another PAT in the fine tradition of prior SV soccer kickers, he was "money in the bank."

But Brad Wilson went on to sell their strengths.

> The Panthers return the equivalent of 18 starters from a 10–2 Colonial League tri-champion squad that lost to Bethlehem Catholic in the District XI Class AAA championship game. Of Saucon Valley's 2,781 rushing yards last season, 2,680 return, 1,715 by Evan Culver. All of the 1,339 passing yards from quarterback Zach Thatcher return. And 1,214 of those receiving yards come back, courtesy of Nate Harka, Mike Kane, Culver, and Mike Paolini. The entire line that blocked for all that production—the entire line.

Get goosebumps reading that quote? We were looking at a dream team. This town, this school, this season, these players. Their time was now. Two players on this team had produced more than two thousand yards of offense. And think about the Hogs, for without their relentless efforts, this offensive production would come up much shorter.

Back to Wilson's article.

> Complimenting their star running back, Mike Kane said that he sees "a lot of improvement in Culver," a scary thought for Colonial League defenses given that he ran through their lines averaging 8.8 yards per carry as a Junior. Did I mention his entire line returned with championship experience? It's a running back's dream. The Panthers, in short, are as loaded as Santa's sleigh on Christmas Eve."
>
> Quoting a humble but laser-focused Head Coach Evancho, "We're not hiding anything, but in no way do I think there is a clear-cut favorite in the Colonial League. I think it will take until Week Ten to determine who the champion is."
>
> "If we stay healthy and stay focused, we can accomplish

even more than last season," Culver said. "The biggest thing for us is to keep our mental focus. No matter what happens, we can't let anything get to us. We can't make mental mistakes."

Kane, the big tight end said, "It's all within our own hands. We have to just come out and work as hard as we can and be the best team we can be every game. If we do that, winning will take care of itself."

Sophomore defensive back/wide receiver Alstan Wolfe added his own take saying, "We can be amazing, but we have to go one week at a time. It's an exciting time for Saucon Valley football."

Mr. Wilson, among other observers of Colonial League football, anticipated an awful lot of winning for these Panthers.

One last bit of advice from Head Coach Evancho: "We need to see a lot of leadership from our Seniors. We have to fine-tune a lot of things from last season. And we have to be able to take steps forward every week."

The preseason hype about this team was a far-cry from years gone by, where the Panthers thundered along running the football with a rather mediocre win-loss ratio.

Let's see how well their predictions played out.

This year, after a week of grueling two-a-day practices in August, with less than desirable temperatures and humidity, the Saucon Valley football team was treated to a season-opening scrimmage under picture-perfect weather conditions.

While football teams across the Lehigh Valley concentrated on their own development, this team took some lumps in preseason form, having a little trouble dispatching Fleetwood. The reigning Colonial League football cochamps dominated on both sides of the ball before walking away with a lopsided victory.

The following week, Saucon Valley faced off against a bigger Dieruff squad in their final preseason test before the regular season opener. The Allentown visitors, competing in the bigger, faster, tougher East Penn Conference, gave the Panthers a glimpse of challenges to come. Coach Chromczak got a little worried during this scrimmage. Despite a few minor stumbles, the scrimmage served its purpose and left the coaching staff generally feeling positive.

There's no secret that the Panthers brought a high-octane offense to the field, which could score bunches of points in a hurry. Led by senior signal-caller Thatcher, Saucon did not disappoint, scoring four touchdowns and punting only once.

But it was the prowling Panther defense that was most impressive.

This was our first big competition of the season against a school with those bigger players. They weren't a powerhouse team and weren't respected in their league, but they were big and had their own Division I candidate. Devante Robinson was their workhorse, who would post a couple of two-hundred-plus-yard games through the regular season along with more than 1,300 rushing yards. That's good competition to get while preparing for the regular season. You don't see that kind of size, athleticism, and skill in the Colonial League often, so it was a good tune-up for the Panthers.

As we'll see throughout the year, we had a good eleven players on both sides of the ball that came to be overpowering at times. That's something we were very good at—playing four quarters of football and just grinding away.

Dieruff's offense was checked all night long in this scrimmage, running only a total of twenty offensive plays. The Panther "D" attacked the Huskies on their way to a dominating shutout, allowing only two first downs (one on a pass interference penalty). Forcing a couple of turnovers, the Saucon Valley defense refused to let Dieruff cross the midfield stripe.

With the final preseason game complete, the Panthers emerged like a finely tuned machine. All pistons were firing—ready to hit the road and chase Colonial League glory.

As a reminder, the three main goals of the season were to:
1. Win the Colonial League
2. Beat BECA
3. Win the District XI Championship

Pink Panthers, Photo credit: Laura Zaharakis

Lady "Pink" Panthers
Remember Coach Evancho's exhortation to the players to have fun? He made sure the coaches and players started out with a pleasurable experience. So stepping back fourteen days into the dog days of August, the moms, coaches, and players went to *boot camp* together!

As reported faithfully each week by Reporter Keith Riefenstahl for *Saucon Source*, the following account tells the tale,

> Two weeks before the regular season began, the whistles were blowing and the coaches were growling on the Saucon Valley High School football field. All the action was at the first 'Lady Panther Camp,' which was specially organized by HC Evancho for football moms, grandmoms, stepmoms, aunts and other women connected to Panther football. Staff and players provided

an up-close, very personalized look at the game of football and what the players endure in order to step out onto the field in their Panther red and black uniforms. Panther Mom Kim Kemmerer said, "Even though high school trainers were on hand as a precaution for the 30 Lady Panther Camp participants, they weren't needed." It was truly an evening filled with fun and learning." Karen Kane had a lot of fun, "We had T-shirts made up and I just remember trying really hard not to embarrass myself. I remember Michael saying to me, 'You did okay Mom.' It was nice quality time with our sons. Didn't actually play a game, we just went through their drills, like, we would go to the different stations. The coaches and players worked the stations and told us what to do and how to go through the drills. It was well attended."

Riefenstahl is deeply-rooted in sports fandom. A freelance writer and former coach, he graduated from Penn State, is a veteran educator, and is a huge fan of Saucon Valley Football. He wrote pregame, postgame, and human-interest stories throughout the season. Much of the game-day material in this book comes, with approval, from Keith's writings in *Saucon Source*.

The *Morning Call*, *Lehigh Valley Live*, and *Saucon Source* report on the high school football scene throughout the year. *Saucon Source* is the only one of the three considered to be a hometown Saucon Valley news outlet. Every week, Keith would be fond of saying, "Come on out and support your home town Panthers. We hope to see you there!"

CHAPTER 5

TUNE UP GAMES

As a team, we left a season full of memories that the entire community can cherish forever. We beat a lot of teams that people said we didn't stand a chance against. It felt like we gave everything we had each and every week, and that hard work paid off. For a small town like Hellertown, it gave people hope that we don't need recruits. Homegrown talent was enough to beat anyone that lined up against us.
—Adam Hough, Saucon Valley Panther (2012–2015)

THE SAUCON VALLEY Football Club, made up mostly of the parents, hosted a weekly pregame Thursday night dinner in the school cafeteria all season, and they also brought in an ice cream truck to serve up welcome relief from the exhausting workouts.

Ryan Meyers shed light on the Thursday ritual. "Every Thursday night we would have a walk through—no pads—just a light work out and mental exercise preparing for the upcoming game. We showered up quick then the parents were nice enough to get together and cook up something special. We'd all go into the cafeteria and there'd be one big long line. It was a requirement, but definitely didn't feel like something we had to do. Everybody's mom had something that everybody liked. And they would bring their best dish. A lot, *a lot* of pasta, you know, gotta get the carbs in for the game. But nobody wanted to miss it. It was just everybody. We'd sit together and have a great time! It was just a good family atmosphere."

Football Booster Club

Barb Thatcher, secretary of the Football Booster Club, offered this insight:

> We had a lot of volunteers. We provided the Thursday evening pregame meals at the school cafeteria, and the kids really looked forward to it. We prepared a lot of great food that the parents brought in. All the parents would sign up each week using that SignUpGenius app. The Meyers family would do brisket and the boys loved that. Michael Kane's mom was famous for her buffalo mac and cheese, which the kids really loved. There was so much more. We really fed them well. We also had a huge fundraiser every year with the basket bingo. The boys would help us by going around to different businesses and ask for donations of gifts or money from area business. That was successful and they liked doing that, wearing their football jerseys. Each week, we also drew a couple of tickets for winners and each week the prize got bigger. That was always in the springtime. We would also buy them shorts and T-shirts for the summer. Even the kids that didn't do the seven-on-seven tournaments got T-shirts and shorts too.
>
> Those were always really good profitable fundraisers. Always had a lot of support from the community with donations, so we rarely had to put any money into it. Those were our two big fundraisers. Bingo always went over really well. We'd sell out every time. That money would go to the year-end banquet. One year, Coach Evancho called the numbers, and he did a really good job! So that was always a lot of fun and very successful. Some of those businesses then turned around and became big supporters. We printed up promotional banners and stuff for the businesses that would support us every year. Those

banners would be hung up throughout the football season in the stadium, facing the crowd. Money raised went toward the year-end banquets where the boys were given jerseys, plaques, and other items for different awards. We would get Fatheads for the senior boys every year. A lot of times after the big basket bingo fundraiser, if there were flowers and plants leftover, several of the boys would take them down to the senior center and hand them out to the residents and patients.

One special event every week was when the [Stephen] Good family made smoothies for the guys. It became a tradition that the boys looked forward to. We would get together and decorate their school lockers with balloons, small signage, pictures—anything to liven it up. We'd go up to the football field into their locker rooms and decorate those lockers as well. We decorated Polk Valley Road, especially when they went to different playoff games. We took it all the way down to Main Street. There were huge gatherings, and the police would provide escorts, with sirens and flashing lights, out of town for away games. Then the police would escort the team buses back in on their return.

Paul Kane, Karen's husband and Football Booster Club treasurer, said, "The concession stands were run by the Saucon Valley Booster Club. They covered all sports. Once we got into the playoffs, the moms would get together and decorate the street every week with balloons and streamers, so the boys would see it all on their way to and from out-of-town games. We would go and see the bus off. During the state playoff games, police and fire made a lot of noise escorting the buses. People lined the streets, showing a lot of spirit. That was something, all the community support. A lot of businesses put up signs like, McDonald's and the Lutheran church across from Neighbors."

There was a core group of moms that would put on the pregame dinners. Every week a different grade was responsible for the food. But a core group of moms—Brenda Carvis, Barb Thatcher, Kim Kemmerer, Karen Kane, and Barb Thatcher—were usually there. They set up the tables and mixed-up giant containers of Gatorade, lemonade, and iced tea. They cleaned up afterwards too! Some parents had different things that the kids looked forward to, their favorite dishes. There was a mom whose son had played football a few years before. She had her catering business supply one of the meals. Barb fondly remembers, "You know, it was worth all the work . . . it was just great memories."

Now it's time to dive in to the 2015 season. Every game is described here but not always in chronological order. This part of the book is essentially divided into three parts.

Part I: Number One is Walking—this section kicks off by chronicling Saucon Valley's encounters with the league's lower-ranked teams. We recognize the contribution of every opponent, as each played a role in the 2015 season's narrative. While these games are presented in chronological order, there will be some gaps separating them from contests against the higher-ranked teams covered in Part II. Despite their valiant efforts, the lower-tiered teams ultimately fell short against Saucon Valley's superior talent.

Part II: Battles Against the Elite—dives into the heart of the season, chronicling Saucon Valley's clashes with the Colonial League's powerhouses. These high-caliber opponents, all contenders for postseason glory, presented fierce challenges. Postseason play was on tap for all.

Part III: The Crucible of the Playoffs—takes us into the white-hot intensity of championship football. Each game presents a new set of daunting challenges, unexpected revelations, and a constant need to evaluate the next hurdle.

Let's Go!

The coaching staff was united. Game plans had been methodically crafted and etched in the minds of the players. Preseason scrimmages were a blur of calculated plays and tactical adjustments.

But now, a pristine field had been meticulously mowed and marked with anticipation in white chalk lines. The chain gang emerged with a silent promise of order. Officials huddled with the coaches, final details whispered before the storm. Then, the captains—leaders and warriors all—took center stage for the coin toss. The air was ripe with expectation.

The game was about to begin.

The band marched onto the track in their familiar strut with their opening number the fans had all heard so often: "One More Time."

Gail Nolf, the voice of Saucon Valley football, with her distinctive and rhythmic voice heard loud and clear from Montford Illick Stadium since 1992, began.

Gail commanded in the press box and made her familiar pregame announcements. "Good evening ladies and gentlemen and welcome to Saucon Valley High School, home of Panther football. Tonight's contest is a PIAA sanctioned event . . . and, HERE COME YOOOOOOUR PANTHERS!"

Led by their head coach, running out onto the field through a phalanx of cheering students and band members, carrying their American flag, the team circled up. The boys all removed their helmets and faced the flag. Gail resumed, "All who are able to, please rise and remove your caps to honor our country and those who serve it with the playing of our National Anthem." The guest singer was announced and intoned the National Anthem. The crowd was ready to soak up another Friday night of Panther football!

All systems GO!

Chills.

"Thundering Herd," Photo credit: Keith Riefenstahl, *Saucon Source*

PART I

NUMBER ONE IS WALKING!

AUTHOR'S NOTE: *Number One Is Walking is a term used on movie sets to indicate the whereabouts of the lead actor. An assistant director announces "number one is walking" to let the crew know the star is leaving the set. In context of this account, the term reflects on the Panthers' collective careers as the lead actor in the 2015 Colonial League season.*

CHAPTER 6

NORTHERN LEHIGH BULLDOGS

We weren't as good as we thought we were.
—Mike Kane, Saucon Valley Panther (2012–2015)

THE PANTHERS TURNED their focus on Northern Lehigh for their Week Two home opener. The Bulldogs won a 20–7 victory over Pen Argyl in Week One and had a little extra incentive when they stepped off their bus in Hellertown on Friday night.

Making a notable reference to *Rocky* the movie, Reporter Keith Riefenstahl gave us a sense for how this first home game proceeded. *Rocky* climaxes in the final round of the championship fight with Rocky Balboa and Apollo Creed trading punches and pounding each other to the point of exhaustion. Both fighters fall to the canvas enduring a nine-count, and of course, it is Rocky who dramatically staggers to his feet, claiming the title from Creed.

Smashmouth Football

While there was no title on the line this night, the Panthers and Bulldogs traded blows for the majority of their September 11 rumble.

The first half highlights showed both teams throwing body blows and moving the ball ever so slowly up and down the field.

Instead of the Bulldogs tying the score midway through the final quarter, the Panther attack switched its intensity as the crowd ramped up their voices to watch Thatcher put his legs in motion. Turning on those turbo jets to race eighty-three yards down the home-field sideline, he scored his final touchdown of the night. No one could touch him! The home team "Jungle," a raucous group of students and alumni, made their presence known throughout the game and especially during that signature run by Thatcher. It would not be his last of the season.

With six minutes left in the game and a fourth quarter shutdown defensive performance by Saucon Valley, the Panthers went up by two scores.

Remember Culver's Eastern Conference Championship game-winning interception?

Inside the closing four-minute mark, defensive back Culver stepped up to intercept Northern Lehigh's final pass at the home team's 32 yard line, dashing any hopes of a Bulldog comeback. Culver was having some fun in this game, felt more like himself after the first game of the season, and let loose on the field.

The Panthers punched out two more first downs before stepping into their victory formation and running the clock down.

It was a great high school football game that wasn't decided until midway through the final period—two tough teams battling in the trenches until one stood tall at the end.

Statistically, Culver led all rushers and almost surpassed the whole Bulldog team with 221 yards on thirty-four carries while scoring three touchdowns. Thatcher dazzled everyone with his feet, rushing for 184 yards on fourteen carries with a touchdown, while completing seven of twelve passes for seventy-seven yards. The Bulldogs amassed 222 rushing yards with forty-seven through the air. A true trench game and classic heavyweight bout where muscle, speed, and skill won the night.

In a move symbolic of Rocky, our Panthers dramatically

staggered to their feet at the end and prevailed in a hard-fought 28–14 victory. The final score doesn't really describe this game, as it could have gone either way before Saucon Valley finally took control in the fourth quarter.

Northern Lehigh ended their season with a 4–6 record, missing the playoffs.

Our Panthers added victory number two, for an undefeated season start.

In this game, Carvis stepped up and became the defensive leader. Throughout the season, he arrived early at every single workout, setting the standard for effort and consistently pushing himself. But whether the other players loved or hated him, Christian was certainly going to let them know when things weren't up to standard. He savored that role, crediting Coach Labatch for instilling in him the confidence to put himself in that position.

Carvis and Kane had both sensed something was still missing after their first game of the season. It came to a head in this Week Two struggle against Northern Lehigh when Saucon Valley didn't take the lead for good until the end of the third quarter.

The following week of practice became an important turning point. "That game," Kane said, "gave us a harsh reality check. We weren't as good as we thought we were."

Small-town America in action: after most games, the players fueled up at the local Waffle House, a postgame ritual that epitomized their high school experience. For Carvis and his "Fab Five" teammates (Kory Kemmerer, Braden Hudak, Culver, and Harka), pregame traditions were equally important. The scent of dill greeted them as they piled into Kory's living room for their pregame ritual. Each one, with a grimace and a laugh, chomped down a pickle before heading out, a reminder that even the toughest games could be faced with a little humor.

Friday after the game typically ended with a bite to eat and a team get-together, often at someone's house to unwind and usher in the weekend. For Carvis, Saturdays meant a well-deserved break, but Sundays saw the Hogs reuniting at Coach Chromczak's home for a double dose of delicious food and film review. These traditions, Carvis reflected, are some of his fondest memories.

"Film study was a cornerstone of our success," Stephen Good recalled. "Every Sunday, the entire offensive line would huddle up at Coach Chrom's house. We'd dissect every play from the previous game. Coach meticulously walked us through each snap, pointing out areas for improvement. He wasn't shy about acknowledging our wins, but he also held us accountable, highlighting our mistakes and outlining clear steps for growth. He'd even sketch out plays on the board, detailing the exact footwork needed. Coach Chrom truly went the extra mile for us."

That was a special invitation-only after-action skull session. It wasn't just the starters who were invited. If a skill player had a really outstanding game, Coach would invite them over to watch film.

What a privilege! Anyone who attended would talk about it for the rest of the year. In fact, ten years later they still talk about how much they learned and how much fun they had.

Ryan Meyers on the Hogs:

> It was a good group of guys. You don't get that very often. We grew up together. We hung out more outside of football than in football. We all have strengths and weaknesses. But we felt like someone's strength would compensate for someone else's weakness. For example, I was on the left side with Cody Zrinski. He was a hell of a football player but didn't exactly always remember his plays. So what I lacked in physical ability he made up for, and what he lacked in memory, I made up for. I recall many times where he would just get into a zone in the huddle and wouldn't listen to the play call. So we're getting into our stance, he would look over and ask me, "What's the

play?" I would say, but he usually couldn't hear me, and he'd ask, "What's the plan?" I would end up pointing at the defender across the line and say, 'Block him.' That's the kind of confidence we had. I didn't mind telling somebody we were coming at them because I knew we were able to pretty much do what we wanted on that line.

Josh Snead always liked the Waffle House. "Yeah, those Friday nights were a lot of fun. Every time I came off the field and passed my parents, they'd ask if I was going to the Waffle House again. Of course! Every Friday night a bunch of us would hang out there." Favorite waffle? "If I was only going for the waffles and a side, I would go with the chocolate chip but if I was getting the all-star breakfast, I would go with the regular waffle and save a little bit of extra room."

CHAPTER 7

CATASAUQUA ROUGH RIDERS

Three things can happen when you pass the football and two of them are bad.
—Woody Hayes, as quoted by Keith Riefenstahl

RYAN MEYERS AND CODY ZRINSKI

Leaders set the standards. When you see two of your best players going full tilt at each other in practice, then you get some of the younger kids thinking, *I can't take a play off because they're not taking a play off.* You see Zach Thatcher break an offensive play in practice and keep running hard the extra thirty yards to make sure he gets to the endzone. The backup quarterback goes in knowing that he's got to try and keep up with Thatcher and push himself to be better. It's interesting when the players are the ones taking accountability. They're the ones pushing each other to keep focused, do their best, play through the whistle. You don't want a coach telling you everything. Defensive coordinator Chris Labatch shared, "That was when it really came to me. I remember me, Matt, and Ed sitting in the coach's office one time thinking for some reason, this just seems a lot easier to coach this year. They're repeating what we would be saying in the last couple of years. They've completely bought into what Matt was preaching." When that happens for a coach, it's pretty easy. He added, "You got a Ferrari, don't wreck it; let these kids play. And that was my philosophy. On the defense, I've got some thoroughbreds over here. I'm gonna let them play and let them be physical. And it worked."

Saucon Valley arrived in Catasauqua on a brisk Pennsylvania evening in late September to battle the Rough Riders during Week Four of this still-young season.

Alumni Field is where I had gotten my baptism in the sparsely appointed press box eight years before this night. Saucon had won that game by a slim one-point score. My daughter attended Lehigh Valley Christian High School just up the road, and the sons of some of our good friends played on that Rough Rider team, so I have fond memories of this place, raw as it was.

This week's challenge for the crew was to remain focused on fundamentals. Don't look ahead to next week's homecoming game against Pen Argyl. Don't let this trap game distract this stalking panther.

Saucon Valley was averaging an astonishing 383 rushing yards per game through the first three weeks of the season.

For those Panther fans awaiting the unveiling of Thatcher's passing game, Riefenstahl reminded us in an article that the late Woody Hayes gave us some perspective with the saying, "Three things can happen when you pass the football, and two of them are bad." Saucon's opponents in the secondary, up to this week, had been very competitive while preventing a wide-open air attack and limiting Thatcher to safe passes.

Sporting a respectable career touchdown passing record of nineteen TDs, Air Thatcher, though grounded, was still a threat. He was smart and didn't make risky throws, as evidenced by his remarkably low interception rate. Alternatively, nobody had come close to shutting down Saucon's ground offensive juggernaut. So, the Panther passing game had not been needed much. Air Thatcher remained on the sideline for most of this game, as in previous contests, although his wide array of receiving weapons did not disappoint when called upon.

The Panthers owned the ground game.

Catasauqua had game-planned to storm the trenches and smother the Panther rushing attack while trying to force Thatcher into airing it out. So eight Rough Riders packed the box on most plays, daring Thatcher to take his chances finding a receiver to catch the ball. That didn't work.

One side note here. Offensive Coordinator Ed Chromczak reminded us that the ground game was the main thing. With a great offensive line, running the ball is the best thing to do.

The Catty defense was led by Ben Nosal and linebacker Tyler Youssef, who both aggressively ran to the ball. Youssef showed decent speed and ran well laterally. They tried to stuff the run with a packed box but without any success. Saucon Valley got comfortable and built up a little lead. Coach Chromczak opened the playbook and created more of a balanced run-pass mix with Air Thatcher finally showing glimpses of what it could be, thrilling Panther fans while frustrating his opponents.

The outcome of this game was never in doubt but saw some drama on the field. Catty learned very quickly that they were in a losing battle. Against the fourth highest-ranked team in the Lehigh Valley they lived up to their nickname. The Rough Riders played too aggressively, resulting in 120 penalty yards, mostly for personal fouls. The game was so chippy, in fact, that Coach Evancho burned two of his first half time-outs to regroup his team and consult with the referees about the illicit tone of the game, seeking protection for his players.

The Roughies tried to sidetrack the Panthers by getting their focus off the game. But for the most part, and in a testament to their leadership both on and off the field, Saucon Valley players took the high road, stuck to their disciplined ways, and went about their gameplan in a workmanlike manner.

Josh Snead made his kicks. Money in the bank.

The thirty-five-point positive margin initiated our first mercy-rule game of the season—it's common nationally for the clock to become a *running clock* (only stopping for timeouts, injuries, etc.) when one team leads by a significant margin, typically in the second half. So, after taking the starters out of the game, Evancho called on his reserves to finish. The junior varsity (JV) mopped up, adding another touchdown when speedy five-foot-six-inch Zach Petiet raced across the goal line on a thirty-nine-yard scoring dash. It was a great opportunity for the Panthers to get some youngsters into a varsity game, and they performed well.

Saucon Valley remained unbeaten after this 55–13 assault on Catasauqua.

Culver solidified his hold on second place in the District XI leader board by adding to his rushing total, now at 760 yards from scrimmage. Closing in on Jamaal Brome of Stroudsburg, he was just sixty-seven yards shy of the district leader, and Culver was tied with Kyle Boney of Emmaus for second in touchdowns scored with twelve. Both players were just one TD behind Antwon Keenen of Bethlehem Catholic and Brome of Stroudsburg. Remember that name: Keenen.

Catasauqua closed out their remaining games with a 1–9 conference record, missing the playoffs.

CHAPTER 8

PEN ARGYL GREEN KNIGHTS

Small Town, Big Dreams. I kept seeing that sign up all over Hellertown and I thought, wow, that was really cool to see how they were really rallying behind their team.
—Joleyce Adams, mother of Evan Culver

THIS HOMECOMING MATCH-UP kept the students in a festive mood. In the lead-up to this game, Saucon held their annual pep rally and bonfire to fuel school spirit. Students and faculty got together to celebrate Panther school pride. Cheers and performances by the band and cheerleaders got everyone excited for the upcoming game. No shenanigans around the bonfire, just clean fun.

It was always exciting, with flames and smoke from burning wood providing a festive atmosphere around a controlled fire with the kids singing, chanting, and having fun together. While burning effigies of rival school mascots is less common today due to safety concerns, the overall experience nurtured a sense of community and tradition already in progress around Saucon.

The Pen Argyl Green Knights rode their buses into Hellertown with a winless record, facing a high-flying Panther squad on the crest of an unbeaten season at the midway point. This was quite a turnaround from previous years, when the tables were turned and Pen Argyl had the dominant advantage over Saucon Valley.

Evancho's team had overcome every challenge they faced so far this year and were now entering the soft part of their schedule. The Panthers' next three opponents had a total of one win and fourteen losses between them. So while Saucon Valley reveled in the homecoming activities that had been taking place all week, they knew this could have all the markings of a "trap" game. Confidence abided with the players and homecoming festivities got the students and fans excited—there was an easy, winnable game on tap. Would the Panthers be caught looking ahead to their Week Nine matchup against unbeaten Notre Dame-Green Pond, the other favorite to win the league?

Answering that question quickly and repeatedly, Saucon did not have to bring their A game to beat these Knights. Evancho's coaching staff had prepared the team to execute well; keeping them focused and disciplined. What a game!

Culver, on this night, became the first player in all of District XI that season to break the one-thousand-yard rushing mark. Seemingly unstoppable, he had rushed for 1,039 yards at just the halfway point of the regular season. Scoring sixteen touchdowns that season, Culver had already become the school's greatest running back. He would eventually hold a school record forty-five touchdowns and rush for 3,042 yards during his high school career. Today he is always the first one to credit his offensive line, the Hogs, with his success and ability to run through those open holes. "Man, that was the coolest thing I've ever watched from my junior and senior years. Look at the relationships we had with each other; I wanted them to succeed as much as they wanted to see me succeed. Look at the relationships they had with each other. It's awesome the way they fed off of each other; that was cool to be a part of."

The Morning Call reported:

When Evan Culver found out he would be a finalist for Saucon Valley's Homecoming King last weekend, the Colonial League's leading rusher quickly asked one of the Queen candidates if he could be her partner for the school's pep rally and to Friday night's halftime ceremonies at Illick Stadium.

The girl he asked, Carli Ziegler, is a wheelchair-bound senior that "everyone in the school just loves," Culver said.

"She's always fun to be around," Culver said. "So when I found out we were both in the court, I asked if she'd allow me to walk in with her."

"I never thought I'd even be nominated for Queen, and I especially didn't think he would ask to be my partner," said Ziegler, who has cerebral palsy and has been confined to a wheelchair her entire life. "I just thought it was really cool for him to ask me."

Naturally, the record-setting running back, who has led the football team to six straight wins, and the popular Ziegler were crowned Saucon Valley's Homecoming King and Queen. That's when Ziegler promptly turned the tables on Culver, asking him if he would accompany her to the Homecoming dance the next night.

"I was honored when she asked me," Culver said of the invitation.

That's the character we see in leadership and friendship.

The Panther Defense on the Prowl

On the field, points came early and often! Led by a relentless defensive and offensive line that made it look like varsity against JV, seven different Panthers combined for ten touchdowns, giving the home team a memorable 67–0 homecoming victory.

It was nearly perfect for the Panthers as they produced twenty-three first downs. The ground game can't get much better than thirty-nine carries for 394 yards. Air Thatcher's receivers caught seven of seven passes for 150 yards. Mastery! The offensive production combined with the shutdown defense simply dominated from the opening whistle.

This might have been Saucon Valley's most complete game of the season.

***

Pen Argyl finished out the season with a conference record of 2–8.

King and His Queen, Photo credit:
Joleyce Adams, Evan Culver's mother

CHAPTER 9

WILSON AREA WARRIORS

It was a very unique dynamic, which I've only seen a handful of times in my football career.
—Chris Labatch, Saucon Valley defensive coordinator

SAUCON VALLEY RODE their momentum to a rare Saturday afternoon game at Wilson Area High School in Week 7. Kickoff for the Wilson game was scheduled for 1:30 pm and the weather was spectacularly good. Nothing but blue skies, a packed press box and free pizza for the crowd handling the announcing, game clock, and the statistics. Russ Lipari, the voice of Wilson Athletics, made a great host along with offering his always-excellent running game commentary.

All the Panthers I interviewed preferred playing under Friday night lights, but Wilson was one of two schools in the Colonial League without lights on their field, so their home games were always on Saturday afternoon. It threw the momentum of the week off by adding an extra day between games on the front end and shortened the following week's preparation by one day.

Prior to this day's kickoff, superstar tailback Evan Culver

had become the third all-time leading rusher in Saucon Valley football history, a record set two years earlier by his running mate and mentor, Nick Savant. By this time, Savant was continuing his successful football career at Muhlenberg College.

Fullback Mike Paolini was also running impressively this season, averaging close to eleven yards per carry.

Thatcher was always a dual threat commando, demonstrating his knack for making big plays on his feet as well as flexing his throwing arm. Thatcher was coming off his best passing game and had completed thirty-one of fifty pass attempts for 534 yards on the season while passing for six touchdowns. He wasn't the District XI passing leader and ranked low on the district quarterback leader list, but his numbers were extremely effective, thus making him a credible dual threat every time he got the ball in his hands.

Thatcher's main target had been "Mr. Human-Highlight," Nate Harka, who was voted the Lehigh Valley's best receiver on Lehighvalleylive.com after the previous week's game. With 116 yards and two TDs the last Friday, Harka sat just two yards from a coveted one-thousand-yard career.

Averaging 470 total yards and forty-four points per game, the Panther juggernaut was loaded with offensive talent behind arguably the best, most disciplined offensive line in the Lehigh Valley. They didn't make many mistakes and saw few penalty flags thrown against them.

Saucon Valley ran one offensive play at the beginning of the Wilson game, scoring what resulted in the game winning touchdown, given the final score. But they had another forty-seven minutes left to play the rest of the game (A PIAA high school football game consists of four quarters, each twelve minutes long). When Bret Comp had led Wilson just a few years prior, that kind of offense was what you could expect from his Wilson team. But as mentioned earlier, both Coach Comp and Coach Evancho had moved on, and the current Wilson team had not reclaimed their former dominance in the Colonial League, while Saucon Valley was on the rise.

During this game, the Panthers amassed total yardage of 606 yards on thirty-five plays, wasting no time at all triggering the mercy rule. Three minutes into the 2nd quarter, Thatcher scampered ten yards into the Wilson end zone to bring the score up to 34–0. Snead converted the PAT to make it 35–0. Mercy rule declared. With Thatcher resting, one more late-first-half pass from reserve quarterback Brandon Holub to Kane along with the PAT by Snead and we finished up scoring for the first half. The Panthers had needed only eighteen plays to rack up seven touchdowns. Holub, with reserves on the field, would carry the ball in for another touchdown early in the fourth quarter to wrap up scoring.

Wilson ran a total of sixty plays but could only add up fifty-five total yards. Panther scoring was shared by Culver, Thatcher, Holub, Harka, Kane, and Snead.

* * *

Wilson finished out their 2015 campaign with a 1–9 record, missing the playoffs for the sixth year in a row. Boy, did they miss Comp and Evancho!

CHAPTER 10

BANGOR SLATERS

*Ability is what you're capable of doing.
Motivation determines what you do.
Attitude determines how well you do it.
—Lou Holtz, College Football Hall of Fame Coach*

FEASTING OFF A domineering seven-win season, the Panthers returned home after thumping Wilson to take on the winless Bangor Slaters. Could a third shut-out in a row fall in our laps, or would this be the dreaded "trap-game" to slip one in the loss column? The Slaters represented one last hurdle to clear before the much-anticipated faceoff with undefeated Notre Dame-Green Pond.

Maybe not. Bangor had produced a total of two touchdowns so far in seven contests. Both touchdowns came during blowout losses to Palmerton and Salisbury.

Against the Slaters, Culver touched the ball seven times, scoring five touchdowns. No worries. This game was a gimme.

Culver amassed a total of 242 rushing yards, averaging thirty-five yards per carry. The Panthers followed Culver to a 61–13 victory. It just did not seem to make a difference who carried the ball. The result was the same.

TOTAL CONTROL. Junior Nate Kehs was Culver's primary backup. He carried the ball six times for sixty-seven yards, averaging eleven yards per carry.

TOTAL COMMAND. Sophomore Steven Rose was Keh's backup. He carried eight times for seventy-four yards, averaging over nine yards per carry.

TOTAL DOMINATION. Air Thatcher, throwing five of five for 122 passing yards, connected on an eighteen-yard touchdown pass to tight end Kane. Harka was the recipient of three other Thatcher passes for eighty-seven yards, averaging twenty-nine yards per catch.

TOTAL AUTHORITY. Throughout the season, Harka made big plays much bigger with his athleticism. That's why Riefenstahl called him "Human Highlight Reel" Harka.

It was a TOTAL POWER PLAY all night long—TOTALLY FUN!

This dominating offensive exercise by the Panthers was highly entertaining for the home crowd, not so much for the visiting team and their fans.

Not to be outdone, the Saucon Valley defense was equally dominant. They played lights-out defense while giving up only 141 yards and eight first downs to the Slaters. Saucon's defense also claimed five takeaways. Sophomore cornerback Alstan Wolfe grabbed two interceptions while Ryan Meyers, Joe Naiburg, and Curtis Clifford each claimed a fumble recovery.

Bangor was able to get on the scoreboard with a couple of late fourth-quarter touchdowns by starting running backs Jesse Rocco and Saivaughan Vass against the Panther reserves.

All said and done it was a punishing performance by the Saucon Valley Panthers.

Talking about Coach Evancho's discipline, Stephen Good remarked, "I think that helped us in the season, because it was kind of ingrained in us—who we are not just as football players, but as young men growing up."

Evancho had built a strong coaching staff. Good went on to mention his offensive coordinator, Coach Chromczak. "He was big on tough love. Like, he would push you to your fullest potential. If you mess up, he would let you have it. But he would know you can improve from it. So he took the time to yell at you a little bit. But then he would explain to you what went wrong and how to improve from it. So we rarely made the same mistake twice."

Snead always disliked kicking on turf. And that was the same thing in soccer. The way he struck the football, a graze underneath, he liked having the grass fields. He would always pick out one small patch of grass that was lifted up a little bit higher. He had a ton of faith in his snapper (Meyers) and holder (Wolfe). Every time the ball was snapped, it hit that same patch of grass. His dad was his greatest influence, especially from a sports perspective. He was the one really encouraging Josh to go out and kick. From a young age, his father was always coaching and pushing him to be better and give all the effort he could. He was also influential in Josh's decision to join the football team. Josh mentioned, "He would always say 'You get home from soccer practice and have so much time left to the day, why don't you go kick?' I took my work ethic from him as well, again, because he was coaching every sport that I participated in at all different levels and on weekends. So he gets home from work tired and goes outside to coach me and my brothers, putting in a lot of time with us."

* * *

Bangor was on the receiving end of that discipline from Snead and the entire team, finishing up the year at 1–9.

PART II

BATTLES AGAINST THE ELITES

CHAPTER 11

SALISBURY FALCONS

"The Jungle" was a huge driving force for some of those kids because, you know, they cheered them on and they would travel.
—Jim Thatcher, father of Zach Thatcher

THE REGULAR SEASON'S first game began with a short road trip through Upper Saucon Township to Allentown for the opening kickoff at Salisbury High School.

The 2014 edition of this Salisbury game had witnessed Saucon squeaking by in a late game surge of Falcon points, by the ever so slim margin of three points, for a final score of 39–36. A determined Falcon team had piled up twenty-two fourth quarter points and threatened to take the Panthers down.

Preparing for the worst and working hard to be the best, the '15 edition of the Panthers needed to treat these Falcons, on their home turf, with respect. The season opener had the potential to be another shootout between two accomplished veteran quarterbacks. The winner would be positioned temporarily on the inside track for a Colonial League title.

In his weekly *Saucon Source* column, Keith Riefenstahl built expectations for each game. He often opened with a prescient metaphor. This time, it was his reference to *Friday Night Lights*, that iconic movie about the Odessa Texas Permian High School football Panthers. He said of the contest at Salisbury, "A week one match-up rarely gets better than this, as both teams have an extraordinary amount of talent and skill. Each team is also part of the preseason championship chatter."

How did it turn out? It was a whole lot of fun watching "King Kong" Cody Zrinski battle "Godzilla" Brett Sonntag. Between them, six hundred pounds of meat and muscle. Definitely worth watching!

In their 2015 opening week campaign, the Panthers withstood initial Falcon pressure and prevailed with a lopsided 39–15 victory to start the season. Saucon did a better job of playing disciplined, clean football and taking care of the ball. However, although they limited their turnovers to a single interception and one fumble recovery, drive-killing penalties interrupted the flow of the game.

The big boys up front, a.k.a. the Hogs, took over the game, pushing and shoving their way to twenty-four first downs and 468 yards of total offense while protecting their quarterback. The Hogs denied the Falcons by not giving up a single sack. But this was week one. Mistakes were made and needed to be corrected. Offering praise for the Hogs, as he had so often throughout the 2014 and 2015 seasons, Culver said, "The sky is the limit for our line, their improvement has been remarkable."

Despite rushing for 147 yards and two touchdowns on twenty-four carries, Culver considered this to be his worst game of the season. He was adjusting to a bulkier physique developed over the summer, which led to some pregame jitters and a lack of comfort on the field. "I came in with high expectations," Culver said, "but it was a learning experience." The strong blocking of the offensive line certainly aided his performance. Meanwhile, fullback "Big Mike" Paolini also had a solid night, grinding out seventy yards and a touchdown on just nine carries.

Showing a balanced attack, Thatcher followed the offensive

line on his legs for sixty-two yards in nine sprints and his first touchdown of the season.

The pass protection provided by the Hogs allowed Air Thatcher to do some damage by completing seven of sixteen passes. Harka earned Offensive Player of the Game for his athletic catches and runs. He made his quarterback look so good with those acrobatic catches! Saucon held Salisbury's talented trio of running backs to only fifty-four yards on the ground for the night. QB Tevon Weber torched the Saucon secondary, however, by throwing for 239 yards and one touchdown, completing sixteen of twenty-six passes and showing that work still needed to be done in that secondary.

The Panther defensive wall was stout, allowing nine first downs all night along with only fifteen points. The entire Saucon defense was recognized for their tenacity throughout the night. Cocaptain and linebacker Carvis played a great game and was all over the place on defense. Credited with eleven tackles, he earned Defensive Player of the Game honors.

When you see good athletes in action, you think they've worked hard to get that way and must have had some inborn ability to do that job. That's partially true in Carvis's case. His first shot at linebacking didn't go well. He was not personally a fan of the linebacker position. But he says now, "I didn't know what I didn't know." He was young and stubborn. Coach Labatch was a tremendous influence. He did a fantastic job of coaching Christian, getting him to a point where he actually believed in himself as a linebacker and believed he could excel at the position. Coach Chromczak was also a great influence. Carvis says, "He and I would butt heads every so often because it was his way or the highway. And well, I was young and stubborn." It worked out well! Carvis expressed nothing but respect and love for him as a coach.

Tight end Michael Kane found help improving his game within his family. His cousin coached the middle school team in 2015. Every Saturday he would hold practice for his team. Afterward they would go to Kane's home and play some pool together. Between his dad, cousin, Mike, and neighbor and teammate Tim Weaver, they would hash out the whole Friday night game together—every play of the game.

Coach Evancho did a tremendous job of putting the right people in the right spot. One remark Coach Evancho echoed throughout that season was that there were times when he really didn't have to coach, constantly giving all the credit to his coaches and players.

* * *

Salisbury would go on to finish the season at 7–3 (Conference) and 7–4 (Overall), losing to Northwestern Lehigh in their playoff game.

CHAPTER 12

THE BACKYARD BRAWL

It was one of the first times in my life that I had a coach that really, truly, truly believed in me. I mean, I didn't play linebacker until my sophomore year of high school. So even then I was kind of back and forth. I was still sort of the linebacker that wasn't, till my junior year. —Christian Carvis, Saucon Valley Panthers (2012–2015)

NEXT UP, THE Southern Lehigh Spartans. Unbeaten and united, the Panther pack bussed down SR-378 to Coopersburg where our archnemesis waited. There, on that grass battlefield, a clash of titans would decide the season's fate.

Every player knew Head Coach Evancho had this rule: Be on the bus at a certain time, ready to go. If you're not on the bus, you will get left behind.

He'd gotten that from Bret Comp, the Marine veteran, when they coached together at Wilson. Strong, sometimes harsh discipline to be learned.

In Matt's universe, the buses never left at a standard time. He would pick an odd time to start, like 4:12, if he wanted the bus to leave at 4:15. He'd tell the kids the bus leaves at 4:12 because they would not forget that specific time. It would stick in their minds. This was part of his discipline from the beginning of the year. When that time came around, the bus closed the door and pulled out with you or without you; with everything you remembered and leaving behind anything you forgot.

So before the biggest game of this young season, Evan Culver was in the training room with Amy, the athletic trainer, getting taped up and ready for the game. Some other kids had gotten in there before him and Evan, ever humble, waited his turn. Then it was 4:12; the bus doors closed and they were off! The players start hollering, "We're missing Evan!" Coach said, "Guys, I told you, we're not waiting for anybody. The bus will not wait. If I'm late, the bus leaves without me." The bus would not wait for anyone.

Amy wasn't happy with Matt. He told her, "Amy, I'm not mad at you. I'm not mad at Evan. I'm not mad at anybody. You knew the time we were leaving. It's all about preparing yourself and managing your time. Manage your time to have everything done before we have to scramble onto the bus."

On Thursdays, he would tell the guys, "Go into the locker room, pack your bags, make sure everything you need is in your bag. Check cleats, pants, girdle, shoulder pads, helmet, chin strap, buckles, belts, laces, anything coming loose, anything about to break. Fix it tonight." He had a list prepared that everyone went through. He would go down this list every pregame, the same list. So on game day, no one had to worry about anything but playing a game. And time was one of those check points. It sent a message that it didn't matter who missed the bus. It didn't matter if they were a coach, a starter, a captain, or anyone else.

Amy drove Evan over to the Southern Lehigh High School field. He didn't play in the first quarter. No player ever missed the bus again at Saucon Valley under Matt's watch.

Special consideration was given to Josh Snead, the kicker. He split time between the school soccer and football teams. On days leading up to game day, Snead would practice with both the soccer and football teams. He attended all soccer practices and games before ending up at football on Thursday, leaving for football about fifteen minutes early to join the pregame walk through. Coaches would defer the special teams part of the walkthrough until he arrived. So pretty much at every game he would come straight from soccer and straight onto the field after changing clothes in the car, riding from one venue to the next.

Some of his practices were pretty grueling, so he got to the football field fatigued. One close call came after a soccer game at Northwestern Lehigh in New Tripoli. As soon as the game was over, he jumped in the car with his family and got dropped off at the gates of the Southern Lehigh football stadium as the National Anthem was playing. He almost missed kickoff.

Of course most fans, not knowing what was going on, were concerned when the ace kicker showed up late and the star running back didn't walk onto the field until the second quarter.

The battle-tested Spartans from Coopersburg had recently crushed Wilson Area High School with their own mercy-rule 44–0 victory. And Southern Lehigh had dominated their rivalry with Saucon Valley football in 2012 and 2013, winning both games by a wide margin (73–7 total). However, the tide had turned in 2014. Saucon Valley emerged victorious twice, edging out the Spartans by a single score each time (30–22 in the regular season and 20–17 in the District XI AAA semifinal). This year's matchup continued the tradition of close games, featuring a fierce battle at the line of scrimmage with explosive offensive displays from both teams. The cochamps from the previous year took the field and the fireworks began.

Evan Culver came into this contest in third place on the District XI rushing leader board. While not yet on the District XI quarterback leader board, Zach Thatcher was also piling up yardage as he, seemingly at will, threw and ran the ball all over the field.

Smart money on this game would have been on Southern Lehigh based on history and revenge for last year. But hedge your bets with the team of destiny, though.

Southern Lehigh tried to stop the potent Panther rushing attack, risking that Thatcher wouldn't cause too much damage through the air.

The Spartans 4-3 defense with active defensive sets tended to be successful. Southern Lehigh dominated Wilson in their game by allowing only four first downs during a shutout effort. However, in their opening night against Palisades, the Spartans had given up almost three hundred yards of total offense and sixteen first downs to the Pirates. Palisades was able to move the ball effectively with a balanced attack. Panther coaches had watched that game film.

Southern Lehigh chose to creep a safety forward in this game, trying to smother the Panther run game. It was obvious who caught everyone's eye when Southern Lehigh broke out of their huddles. Fleet-footed split-end Ethan Price, standing six feet one inch and weighing 180 pounds, appeared much bigger than the players around him. He played bigger in every other game Southern Lehigh had played during the season so far. Price stormed into the 2015 season on opening night by hauling down ten receptions for a staggering 296 yards—a District XI record. Along with three touchdowns to start off the year, he was, for obvious reasons, a favorite receiving target.

Quarterback Blake Levengood pitched to Price often. Levengood had been very accurate in his first games of the season, completing twenty-four of thirty-one passes for 516 yards and leading all District XI quarterbacks, throwing seven touchdowns so far. That included all the AAAA quarterbacks too!

Another Spartan weapon was Tim Walters. Walters was Southern Lehigh's best running-back that year. As a skill player, he was very productive running and catching the ball.

Aside from throwing jump balls to Price, they employed toss-sweeps and sprang Walters outside. Levengood also showed decent running abilities in his own right and frequently moved the chains on quarterback counter plays.

It has been said that familiarity breeds contempt. Two unbeaten teams with a rivalry history squared off to do battle under the lights and laid the groundwork for great entertainment. But we'd been here before and Southern Lehigh had generally owned these contests over the years, so even though Saucon Valley had won the last two contests, revenge on this night was top of mind for the visitors from Saucon Valley.

Thatcher for the Score, Photo credit:
Keith Riefenstahl, *Saucon Source*

When local high schools with a rich history of gridiron battles clash, it becomes more than just a game. This week's matchup between Southern Lehigh and Saucon Valley was a prime example. Nicknamed the "Backyard Brawl," this rivalry went beyond a catchy phrase. Southern Lehigh boasted a consistently strong program, putting up impressive scores in the first two weeks of this young season. But in week three, Saucon Valley countered with a battle-hardened squad forged by tougher competition. The stage was set for an epic clash of veterans on both sides fighting for bragging rights.

> ## MY FAVORITE GAME?
> "The game I think Saucon Valley was viewed as the little brother in week three of 2014, at home against Southern Lehigh, going into the game as we hadn't beaten them in a number of years. We ended up winning a tight game that not many people thought we could win (including some people within the Saucon Valley football community). After this game our team had a swagger that carried us the rest of that season and into 2015. I don't think the success we had in 2015 would have been possible if we'd never gotten over the hump and beaten Southern Lehigh in 2014."
>
> Mike Kane (2012–2015)

The Proud Panther Parent Prediction for this game came from Brenda Carvis: "Thirty one to twenty . . . because the team has great chemistry and is determined to win!"

Southern Lehigh threatened to dominate in the first half. Our Panthers did not disappoint, keeping up with them. Both teams came out ablaze early on, relying on their main weapons, matching score for score. The tone of the game shifted ever so slightly near the end of the first quarter.

The Panther defense stopped the Spartans on their final down series of the first quarter, forcing Southern Lehigh to settle for a thirty-six-yard field goal by kicker Anthony Colasurdo. With the home team up by three, the end of the first quarter scoreboard showed 17–14 in favor of the home team.

Five scores in the first quarter! What's next?

Evan Culver, who'd missed the bus, stood on the sidelines during the entire first quarter and had not touched the ball yet.

The Hogs began to assert themselves in the second quarter, slowing the Spartans down and making them fight harder for any gains. The last play of the half was the killer.

It looked as if the Spartans were going to score and take the lead into the locker room. Levengood dropped back to throw another jump ball to the six-foot Price. However, on the last play, in action reminiscent of his buddy Culver's game-saving snatches against other teams, "Highlight Reel Harka," a full six inches shorter than Price, came up huge with a game-changing interception in the end zone to protect a slim Panther lead.

What a relief and what a way for the visitors to go into the half time locker room!

Offensive fireworks from both teams had characterized the intensely competitive first half. The exhausted fans watched the Panthers hang on to a 28–24 lead. The two teams matched each other well, striking blow for blow, and trading scores that showcased their big-play styles. Quarterbacks Levengood and Thatcher matched each other from one possession to the next.

The wow factor of Price's first half performance was off the charts great! He was impressive, making big plays for his team against Saucon's single coverage, looking unstoppable.

The crowd was ready for a break—some hot dogs and soda. Some needed to stretch their legs and walk around the track. As the halftime band played their favorite marching tunes, this crowd buzzed with anticipation and a lot of trash talk. Conversation in the press box was complimentary of the visitors holding their own but revealed confidence in the home team. The cramped Southern

Lehigh press box was an interesting place to watch a game. The home team assistant coaches climb up a ladder through the roof and stand on top of it to observe the game. They were not happy while making their way down to the locker room and I wisely stepped out of their way. The stage was set for what would prove to be a grand finale. Nobody was leaving this stadium until the clock ran out.

In what would prove to be prophetic, the Panthers played up to their competition and did not disappoint. Head coach Evancho and defensive coordinator Labatch, defensive-minded geniuses and masters at making halftime adjustments, changed the course of this game. The cagey Panthers pounced on their prey during the second half. Their halftime adjustments enabled Saucon Valley to smother the Spartans in the third quarter and hit them hard the rest of the night.

The Panthers rode Harka's momentum-shifting interception into the second half while extending their lead to 35–24 on Thatcher's next touchdown, a nine-yard run. As the lead widened in favor of the visitors, the fourth quarter showcased an open tight end Kane in the back corner of the end zone for a ten-yard touchdown reception.

The Panthers virtually shut down Price and the Southern Lehigh offense the rest of the way. Saucon Valley trapped Levengood inside the pocket and pressured him into hurried decisions more effectively in the second half than the first.

Outplaying Southern Lehigh 21–6 in the second half, Saucon Valley cruised to a three-score 49–30 victory, improving to a 3–0 record while Southern Lehigh dropped to 2–1.

When asked about the strategy to reign in Price, Labatch said, "We just mixed coverages a little more. We showed man coverage on the first two series. We started playing off, then pressing, rolling the coverage, then playing zone. I think all and all we played him well. Culver slipped on one play allowing Price to make a one-handed catch that most athletes can't do anything about."

> **MY FAVORITE GAME?**
>
> "Any game going against Southern Lehigh. School rivals, the students were extra into it with a social media presence. We didn't like them. They didn't like us. The games each year always saw extra activity after the whistle. Always felt good leaving that game as the winner, knowing we owned both sides of town."
>
> **Nate Harka (2011–2015)**

As a team, Saucon rushed for 461 yards on forty-seven carries with Culver scoring three touchdowns and rushing for 207 yards on twenty-three carries (in three quarters of play). Thatcher rushed fourteen times for 156 yards, adding three more touchdowns. Thatcher also completed two of six passes for thirty-one yards, a touchdown pass, and one rare interception.

It was a great team effort by Saucon Valley to remain unbeaten against a very good and always dangerous Southern Lehigh squad. Panther receivers Wolfe and Harka provided exceptional run blocking downfield to help their quarterback and tailback to big runs.

Fullback Paolini made a couple of key runs and one reception out of the backfield.

Big Mike kept the Spartans off balance from an offensive perspective with his blocking and deflated the Spartans from his linebacker position with a key late game interception.

Cody Zrinski rightfully gets three hundred pounds worth of attention for his outstanding defense, but this night Ryan Meyers was a *beast* from his defensive line position right next door to Cody. The two together? As my New Jersey friends are fond of saying, "Faget about it!"

Culver, he ran, he caught, he defended, and he blocked, nailing some *pancake* blocks on the edge to help spring big Thatcher runs.

Nate Kehs, playing his first year as a starting linebacker, stuffed the runners with his defensive "jams" while lending help defending against Price.

As a receiver, Harka obviously enjoyed catching passes. But he also appreciated the opportunity to block for his teammates, especially for good friend Culver. "We had a run-heavy offense, but that didn't bother me," he said. "It was all about winning and we were a team."

Snead, money in the bank as usual, converted all seven point after touchdown attempts.

The offensive units of both teams entertained the crowd with 824 yards worth of outstanding Friday night football! Not bad for a five-dollar ticket.

Price finished week three as the district leader in reception yardage (502) and reception touchdowns with five But the Saucon Valley secondary effectively shut him down in the second half, allowing only one touchdown with 169 yards for the game. Tagging Levengood for two interceptions, the District XI leading passer was held to 241 yards on ten completions. Playing only three quarters, Culver finished week three in second place for the District XI rushing leaders with 575 total yards gained.

Shades of 2014, when both teams finished week three with similar records and ended the season as Colonial League cochamps. Would we see a repeat?

***

The Spartans finished out this season with a 7–3 conference record, winning two more in the Eastern Conference playoffs after beating Jim Thorpe and Allentown Central Catholic.

AUTHOR'S NOTE: *Two coaches and two players from the 2015 team have followed up their Panther careers by taking* *coaching positions at Southern Lehigh. Coaches Phil Sams and Ed Chromczak switched employers two years later after the 2017 season, with wide receiver Alstan Wolfe joining them while still playing for Kutztown University and Cody Zrinski following later.*

CHAPTER 13

PAYBACK!

Everybody's mom had something that everybody liked. And they would bring their best dish. A lot, a lot of pasta, you know, gotta get the carbs in for the game.
—Ryan Meyers, Saucon Valley Panther (2012–2015)

CHRIS LABATCH, TALKING about Northwestern Lehigh and the challenge coming in the next game in Week 5, said, "Harry Hall is their big threat and is as good as advertised. As a unit, they have a be-physical mentality like Northern Lehigh. Their offensive line is big upfront and their QB is an athlete who can run and throw. They like to throw to their tight end with their wide-outs being more than capable of making big plays. We have to play a great game defensively to keep them in check."

Evan Thatcher recalled his worst experience at the Northwestern game in 2014. That was his junior year, when he'd broken his wrist on the New Tripoli field. That had been a terrible game. Saucon Valley couldn't do anything good and got stopped. It was their only loss that year. He remembered running track later on at that same exact stadium and hated it. Off-season surgery was needed to repair the wrist.

This 2015 game was a rematch between two of the three 2014 Colonial League Cochampions, Northwestern and Saucon Valley. The Tigers were the only Colonial League team to beat the Panthers the previous year, sealing that three-way tie at the top.

This next game would be a high-stakes battle on soggy Saucon Valley grass between two very talented teams, hoping to keep their championship and postseason hopes alive. The Panthers had the home-field advantage before kickoff. But this opponent was not to be taken lightly and had a history of owning the competition between these two teams.

With little margin for error, Northwestern would pull out all the stops to avoid their second loss of the season and they'd seemed to have Saucon's number almost every year. The Panthers hadn't beaten the Tigers since 2008, which was the last time the staff from New Tripoli had fielded a bad team—seven years! No surprise that this game was circled on the Panther calendar early on.

Northwestern Lehigh knew Saucon Valley was putting a formidable team on the field, perhaps as good as Notre Dame, who was also undefeated at this stage of the season and who had beat Northwestern during week one.

Northwestern (3–1) had thus far averaged thirty-four points per game while only giving up an average of nine. Strong offense and tight defense make a good winning game formula! The Tiger's three wins came at the expense of Pen Argyl, Bangor, and Wilson, all winless so far this season. All three teams were beaten soundly by Saucon Valley. Northwestern Lehigh was a team that couldn't be overlooked; the Panthers needed to be prepared for a battle.

In his preseason preview of Northwestern Lehigh, Josh Folck of Lehighvalleylive.com said,

> Northwestern football coach Josh Snyder isn't spending much time this preseason talking about how the Tigers won their first District 11 Class AA title in 12 years

last season. With the graduation of some great players including all-state selections Cam Richardson and Taylor Breininger, it's a new team in 2015. Northwestern does welcome back star running back-linebacker Harry Hall, who rushed for 1,800 yards last season and ranks second all-time in program history. He will rush behind an offensive line that returns four starters from a season ago. The Tigers defense has seven starters coming back with three senior linebackers who have started since their sophomore seasons. The defensive line will feature two four-year starters. Safety Dylan Snyder is a four-year starter and the vocal leader of the secondary.

Senior running back and linebacker Harry Hall added, "I think it's in the past. I think we just have to move on and realize we're not the same team. We're going to be running a lot of different stuff this year compared to last year. I think we just have to have some guys step up."

Coach Snyder chimed in, "I said day one, we shared the league and we won the district title but we're not defending anything. No one's going to come into our showcase and steal our banners and steal our trophies, we're not defending it. We're out to earn everything from scratch again this year."

He's emphasizing that past wins don't guarantee future success. Motivating his team to work hard and earn everything, he put everyone on notice that Northwestern had a hungry attitude. They were coming to fight for the win!

Coming into this game, the Panther offense was averaging 465 yards of total yardage per game. They had been exceptional in their offensive run production behind the ever-present Hogs who did what they did best—pave the way, create holes, and push the opposition down the field.

Thatcher was a true dual threat quarterback, having run for seven touchdowns and thrown for three more. Kane had caught a touchdown pass in each of the past two games, bringing him closer to the school receiving touchdown record.

Saucon Valley was laser focused on this opponent, with an unrelenting rushing attack and play-action pass plan designed to keep the Tigers off balance enough to create big Panther plays.

The Tigers' core four-four defense was very good at keeping points off the board. In four games they had given up a total of thirty-seven points. During their only loss against Notre Dame on opening night, they gave up 81 percent of that number. So the Tiger Defense had been playing near-shut-down football since week one.

Josh Folck ends his article by quoting Head Coach Evancho. "Their defense runs to the ball well and plays aggressive. Chet Karpyn is a solid defensive tackle and Harry Hall is a quick linebacker."

Gameday

Northwestern, like other Panther opponents, game-planned to smother the Panther run game. The Tigers matched up and applied man-to-man coverage on the Saucon receivers while committing all other defenders to smother the run.

The Panther receiving corps of Kane, Harka, and Wolfe had to win their fair share of one-on-one battles against the Northwestern secondary.

Looking back to the 2014 game shows that Northwestern had success limiting Saucon's potent offense. In New Tripoli the Panthers were held to eight first downs and only 143 yards of total offense. Northwestern always played tough and anticipated very well. One of Saucon Valley's main plays was a dive option. The quarterback either hands off to the full back or keeps the ball. There were two Colonial League teams that could stop that. Northwestern did it because their coach understood the play. They stunted up front and their defense would stop the play before it got started. So that took out literally 40 percent of our playbook, which was frustrating because we would almost always run that dive option play. Thatcher said, "I would like to say we were trying to get creative, but in the end, I think it was more like 'let's keep running this and whether it's successful or not, changes will get made.'"

The biggest Tiger to tame was senior Hall, rushing for over four thousand yards and forty-five touchdowns scored in his career. He was their playmaker. The last time these two teams met, Hall had run for 240 yards on thirty-one carries and two touchdowns. Coming into this game, he had racked up 618 yards and nine touchdowns. Sitting at number seven on the District XI rushing leader board, he was just 142 yards behind Culver.

Culver Stretching for Gain, Photo credit: Keith Riefenstahl

The Saucon defense had their work cut out against a Tiger offense utilizing a variety of shotgun formations on offense. One time it would be a one-back set; the next time it'd be two. The Tigers played motion and misdirection down the field with some success.

In addition to Hall, quarterback Dylan Snyder threw a lot of passes and used his feet to make big plays.

Two very capable and well-coached teams faced off on a muddy night, adjusting to sloppy field conditions from soaking rains making this a classic grinder. Both squads played a clean game in terms of penalties and turnovers, making it very close all the way to the final buzzer. Fun game to watch.

Culver and Hall somehow cancelled each other out, so it came down to the production of the quarterbacks to make the difference. Which of the two would find their receivers on that soggy night?

Rain gear for the fans was a necessity while the outer bands of Hurricane Joaquin created havoc on the field. Wet and cold. But that didn't stop the hometown Panthers from scoring more points and remaining unbeaten in the face of the Tigers.

The Panthers once again leaned on the Hogs (Good, Carvis, Meyers, Polak, Zrinski) and their unstoppable ground attack to register twenty-six first downs while amassing 436 total yards. Culver followed those Hogs all the way to 283 yards on thirty-two carries, finessing and powering his way to four scores while setting a new Saucon Valley High School record of forty-five career touchdowns.

It was pure football, smash mouth in the mud. Forget long passes, the game was a brutal ground war. Four runs chewed off five yards each, a nine-yard burst, and an eleven-yard dash kept the momentum going, but everything else was a fight for inches in the muck.

The fans in the stands endured the bad weather while rooting for their team.

On one second and goal play, Thatcher had trouble with the slick ball, losing possession to the Tiger defense. So close, yet so far away! That lost fumble cost the Panthers valuable points with a major momentum shift to the hungry Tigers.

Saucon's defense stiffened up on the ensuing series, forcing the visitors to punt for the first time of the night early in the fourth quarter. Carvis, Culver, Kehs, and Thatcher all made critical tackles on that series of downs, limiting the Tigers to a total of only fifteen gained yards.

The next turning point occurred when Kane and "King Kong" Zrinski met at the quarterback, sacking Snyder for a three-yard loss. Momentum now favored Saucon Valley with midfield possession. Tie score. Payback in the wind and on the minds of the Saucon Valley players.

With an undefeated season on the line, a collective hunger pulsed through the Panthers, their every step fueled by the scent of destiny. Thatcher and Culver would be the only two Panthers to touch the ball in the rest of this game.

In familiar control of the ball and the game—running behind his beloved Hogs, Culver was the man of the hour as he ripped off runs of seven, twenty-five, three, ten, eight, and two yards with the last one powering over the left side behind Zrinski and Meyers for a touchdown lunge.

However, Snead's normally certain extra point was blocked, leaving a slight door open for the Tigers to steal a victory with plenty of time remaining on the clock at 00:07:58.

Snead then botched the onside kick, which was recovered by Northwestern's Caleb Clymer at the Northwestern 37 yard line. We'd been here before. The fans were rabid, standing and yelling. It was Bedlam. Crunch-time.

Time was against our side. The seasoned Tiger offense, a well-oiled machine, sprang into action, determined to capitalize on this golden opportunity. But just when it was needed the most, this Panther band of brothers stepped up to the challenge.

The Hogs kept hope alive with sacks, pressures, and passes broken up by a combination of Abe Lugo, Zrinski, Kehs, Harka, Carvis, and the rest of the Panthers coupled with great downfield pass coverage by Wolfe, Kemmerer, and the rest of the Panther secondary snuffing out the Tiger threat, forcing them into their second punt of the evening.

Then, the tables quickly turned a short time later when Saucon was forced to punt after two more first downs. Time was running down, but Northwestern and Harry Hall had the ball and control, sensing their own destiny on the Saucon side of midfield.

At the Saucon Valley 45, Hall took the handoff but was met at the line by the gang of Kehs, Harka, and Carvis. Culver then caught Snyder five yards behind the line of scrimmage, sacking him at midfield. Snyder attempted another pass that was broken up by Kemmerer. Snyder's last-gasp pass was knocked down by Carvis.

With a great feeling of relief, Saucon Valley took over on downs, stepping into their now-familiar victory formation. Thatcher took a knee to end the game.

Saucon Valley emerged victorious in a nail-biting 27–21 win over the last Colonial League team to beat them.

Payback is sweeter the more you have to earn it and our boys remained unbeaten, still tied with Notre Dame on top of the Colonial League.

Time for a well-earned visit to Waffle House.

Thinking back to when this band of brothers began to gel as a team, Wolfe said, "It was this game. It was close! We knew that we were beatable. So we had to practice a little bit harder. We had to lift a little bit more. We had to run a little faster. Like we had to just keep going, keep pushing ourselves. I think we pushed ourselves harder after that game. So we had to make sure we didn't make mental mistakes."

Labatch added what he thought made this team special. "You started seeing who the athletes are and who's got possibilities. Then you start seeing them work with the other players. Thatcher takes a Kemmerer under his wing in practice and explains how we do things. Then once you put the pads on, you see Kory responding. Then, you get it, that Kemmerer's the guy for that position because he shows that he understands it. A kid like Carvis walks a Kehs through the linebacker position in preseason. Tells him, 'This is your responsibility, do's and don'ts, 'you've got to take care of it." And you know, that's when the leadership starts to show. The players started to plug holes as the season progressed. Kids like Holub, who is young, steps up and gets a few reps here and there to give Culver a break. I could put in another D lineman and give Cody a break. It was a very unique time where it all started to mesh. The kids really believed in what we were teaching and the seniors took over in about week three. After that tough game against Northwestern Lehigh, we made the turnaround. We shut out a couple of teams and it was like, okay, these kids really understand what we're doing."

★ ★ ★

Northwestern had cumulatively outscored foes 9,277 to 9,259 in program history dating back to 1965. They outscored opponents the 2015 season 269–133, while losing only to Notre Dame-Green Pond and Saucon Valley. They were the third Panther opponent to eventually march into the playoffs, finishing their season with an 8–2 conference record and splitting their postseason contests to wind up at 9–3 for the year.

CHAPTER 14

COLONIAL LEAGUE GAME OF THE YEAR

I'd have to say the Notre Dame game was my favorite, you know, I mean, that was like a movie.
—Karen Kane, mother of Michael Kane

LABATCH, REFLECTING ON the importance of this game said, "I had many family members living in the eastern part of New Jersey and down south in Pennsylvania who drove up for this game. So you're talking almost forty-five minutes to an hour and a half drive just to see a high school football game. We still talk about it when I see them in person."

MY FAVORITE GAME
Zach Thatcher, reflecting on this Notre Dame game said, "I could never understand why they suddenly couldn't stop us because they obviously had the game film. They knew what we were doing. I don't know why they never adjusted. But that is what made Notre Dame my fun game. Because they couldn't stop that dive trap."

At this point in the season, Saucon Valley was sporting an impressive 8–0 record after beating some of the Colonial League's strongest football programs. Battle-tested and hardened against distractions, Saucon Valley came into the final two league games with one objective in mind, their first goal set out at the beginning of the season—win the league title.

The Notre Dame Green-Pond Crusaders (ND-GP), on the other hand, had built an equally impressive 8–0 record defeating many of the same teams, and dominated their opponents in the same convincing manner as the Panthers. Two bulls would now rush head-long at each other.

Game of the year? Most everyone around the league agreed. The media agreed. Players and coaches agreed. This one would truly be a "winner-take-all" contest.

With two league games remaining on both schedules against lesser competition, this matchup was for the Colonial League Championship. The winner of this game would remain undefeated and have a lock for that trophy with one game to go. So this one was for all the marbles!

At this stage of the season, attested by fans from both teams filling up Montford Illick Stadium in Hellertown, it didn't get any bigger than this. A private school that can recruit players against a public school limited to homegrown talent.

A record crowd packed in. Lots of energy and noise! Smiling faces. The band cranked up their marching tunes. The stadium was jammed with fans in the stands and on the grassy hill. As the Panther squad walked out onto the field before the game, they were surrounded by a phalanx of band members, cheerleaders, students, and all kinds of fans. There must have been in excess of one hundred people on the southern end of the field at that point before the team walked out.

This game would be one for the ages and everyone knew it!

This was the first Panther game in more than a decade where

the Saucon Valley School District Athletic office offered and encouraged advanced ticket sales and there were still some *very* long ticket lines on game night for this showdown.

Wait. This is Notre Dame? They never field an exciting team. For those readers not familiar with the background history, one private school, called Pius X, had closed down the previous year. Their head coach, Phil Stambaugh, had taken a job at Notre Dame-Green Pond as the assistant head coach under longtime head coach, Chuck Muller.

With the closing of the Pius X High School at the end of the 2014–2015 school year, most of their coaches and players, veterans of multiple state championship runs at the single A level, followed Stambaugh to Notre Dame-GP. As a direct result, Notre Dame quickly became the biggest obstacle remaining in the Panther's path.

This one would be better than *Facing The Giants*.

Brad Wilson, writing again for lehighvalleylive.com, talked up this game.

> Getting chemistry right in the science lab makes for a major challenge. It's a tough subject, and sometimes it doesn't come easily. After 2014, Notre Dame coach Chuck Muller knew chemistry could be just as strenuous a feat to accomplish on the football field. "We didn't like each other last year," Muller said. "We had kids coming in from different schools and it didn't work."
>
> "Quite the opposite this season," Muller said. "This year chemistry is absolutely not a problem," he said. "These kids are close." Crusaders Senior Aaron Weller, who attended Pius X last year, agreed. "It's working out really nicely," Weller said. "We're getting really close-knit, like a little family. We're jelling nicely."
>
> The two groups together make a nice recipe. Pius X Royals won 11 games the previous season and was a

perennial district and state playoff contender in their classification. The Royals were a state quarterfinalist in 2014. Meanwhile Notre Dame-Green Pond won no games last season and has gone 12 years without a postseason berth. That will undoubtedly change in 2015.

"We have the winning tradition," Weller said. "The Notre Dame kids aren't used to winning but they bring the desire to win."

Senior Lineman Cody Georges, a Crusader last season, likes the mix. "They bring a good mindset to us," he said. "The only thing that got us through last season was not giving up. We never gave up, that's our mindset. Combine the two and it could well be a winning formula."

What posed a problem for Muller was finding playing time for what was suddenly a richly experienced team. Notre Dame was the only area scholastic team bringing back twenty-one starters. The glut of experience had Muller leaning toward a two-platoon system to make the most of the talent on hand.

One spot where there were no question marks was at quarterback, where senior Tre Jordan had put up Powerballesque numbers at Pius X in 2014: 197-for-296 passing to gain 2,940 yards and score thirty-five touchdowns, along with 779 rushing yards and fifteen more touchdowns on the ground. That's fifty—five-zero—touchdowns from one source. And remember, the mastermind of the offense that Jordan had thrived in—Stambaugh—was now running the offense at Notre Dame-Green Pond.

No wonder Muller said with a smile that his offensive line's main job was to keep Jordan in one piece. "It's a lot of fun to play in this offense," said Georges, who brought 265 pounds to his tackle spot. "But you really have to be conditioned. That's the most important thing."

Jordan didn't lack for skilled athletes catching his passes and receiving his handoffs. Jalen Simpson had averaged 9.2 yards a carry for Pius in 2014, and Crusaders junior Mitch Daniel could carry the ball as well. Jordan had seven or eight receivers all seeing significant playing time.

Elusive chemistry may well have been the only question. Muller said, "How the Crusaders answer adversity will tell that tale." That recipe had made a feast this year as they rolled over their competition much the same way as Saucon Valley had handled theirs.

Senior lineman Edgardo Ferreira said, "We all want the same thing. We want to win all the games, win our medals, go all the way, and win a state championship. We all want to win."

Head Coach Muller added: "I want to play more than ten games this season. We can make the District XI Class AA playoffs for the first time since 2003 if we have a good effort every Friday night. We can see a Game 11 if we do that. This is a special group of kids." Sound words from a man steeped in football reality.

Destiny Night!
The District XI passing leader, Tre Jordan, countered the District XI rushing leader, Evan Culver. Both were explosive and seemingly could score at will. As John Leone said on the RCN broadcast, "Both teams have the guns. It's up to which team has the most bullets. Your heart goes out to Notre Dame. There's a lot of history to be made here tonight. But your head tells ya there's a lot of weapons on that Saucon Valley team. Culver always had the vision to get through holes, but this year he's added the element of power."

The Proud Panther Parent Prediction this time came from Carol Mamay Paolini. "This is going to be a nail biter, but my prediction is SV 28 ND 24. Defense will be the name of the game and SV will dominate! GO PANTHERS!"

Finally, the much-anticipated showdown was here. Could upstart Notre Dame squash Saucon Valley's title hopes? Fortunately for the fans, the game was recorded by both RCN and Service

Electric and it's still thrilling to watch ten years later!

The night air was brisk and clear, with the stars shining brightly over the Lehigh Valley. Two battle-tested and undefeated teams clashed while the "Jungle" ramped up the noise level in the sold-out stadium. TV and radio were on-site covering this as a major event. One of the most talked about games in the Lehigh Valley this year was proving to be all Saucon Valley in the early action. The band jammed, the cheerleaders looked great, yelled, cheered, and did their pushups after every score. In the press box, the glass window rattled as we pounded on the inside while fans outside were pounding on it in jubilation every time the Panthers made a big play or scored. Bedlam reigned in the stands!

Culver on his way to more yardage
Photo credit: Keith Riefenstahl, *Saucon Source*

Despite the pregame buzz about offensive fireworks, the game began with a surprising back-and-forth defensive struggle. Like cautious boxers, both teams spent the first quarter feeling each other out, resulting in a scoreless stalemate. The Panther and Crusader defenses dominated; a fumble here, a foiled fake punt there, trading stops instead of offenses lighting up the scoreboard.

The much-anticipated offensive explosion remained elusive as the clock ticked down to a scoreless first quarter.

Evan Culver is coming to an end zone near you
With eleven minutes and nine seconds remaining in the second quarter, Notre Dame kicked a twenty-one-yard field goal that was flagged for a false start. After the five-yard penalty, ND kicked again but missed, turning the ball over to the Panthers at the Saucon Valley 19 yard line.

All he needed was a little daylight. On the very next play, Culver took a quick-pitch around the left end, found a seam and raced seventy-two yards all the way down to the Crusader 9 yard line, where Jalen Simpson finally caught up to him and brought him down. Two plays later, from two yards out, the Panthers cashed in as the Hogs opened a hole large enough for Culver to plunge through and step into the end zone for the first score of the night. At the 00:09:55 mark in the first half, sure-footed Josh Snead cashed in his first point after touchdown making it 7–0 in favor of the hometown boys. We were thrilled! In the excitement of that explosive drive, we cheered, we hollered, Gail Nolf ran outside the box and yelled her support. The glass rattled. The parents beamed with pride!

Saucon's defense again stiffened on the next Notre Dame offensive series, denying them a single first down. Kevin Dadio punted away and Saucon Valley took over at their own 40 yard line. Behind the Hogs, Culver and Thatcher alternated carries to move the ball back down to the Crusader 24 yard line. On the seventh play from scrimmage, Thatcher kept the ball on his favorite option play. Culver provided the crucial block, and Thatcher burst down the left side of the field for a twenty-four-yard touchdown scramble. With five minutes and three seconds left in the opening half, Snead booted his second point after touchdown of the night and the home team moved ahead 14–0. More hootin' and hollerin' from the crowd! Glass rattled. It looks like another familiar beat-down looming.

The 2015 edition of Notre Dame was not accustomed to this kind of treatment and would answer with their first points of the night only five plays later as Jordan picked apart the Saucon Valley secondary. The Crusader all-star senior quarterback found receiver Jalen Simpson open in the right flat for six. Unfortunately for the visitors, defensive tackle Cody Zrinski broke through the Crusader line to block the extra point, and keep the score at 14–6 in favor of the Panthers. We were thrilled that special teams kept this one in check!

With a strong kickoff return up to the Saucon Valley 39, the home team wasted no time crafting their next scoring drive. The Hogs, followed by Thatcher and Culver, led their team down field, weaving, lunging and powering to move the sticks for three first downs. QB Thatcher then ran a "sweep" around the right end for a five-yard touchdown. Snead kicked his third extra point and gave the ecstatic crowd a 21–6 score going into half time. Smiles all around! High fives throughout the press box.

The Jungle was happy, the band members played their half time show, fans enjoyed the night, and the chatter in the press box was all about the title. Saucon Valley looked strong while Notre Dame was turning out to be a disappointment. But as so often happens with championship caliber teams, something happened in that locker room that changed the mindset of both teams.

Notre Dame kicked off to start the second half and "Prime Time" Alstan Wolfe carried the pigskin thirteen yards up to the Saucon Valley 38—similar ball spot as the last kickoff return. Wash, rinse, repeat.

After trading possessions, Saucon Valley finally moved down field sixty-two yards with Culver and Thatcher taking turns carrying the ball. Thatcher put the icing on the cake with a twenty-five-yard keeper into the end zone for our fourth touchdown of the evening. Snead added another point after touchdown to make it 28–6 with two minutes and thirty-six seconds left on the third quarter clock. Thatcher looked unstoppable in what may have been his best high school game. He eventually rushed seventeen times for 162 yards, scoring three touchdowns for the night. The celebration was starting to gear up—but Tre Jordan was on the field with the ball.

In the cool night air, he brought Notre Dame back while leading an eleven-play Crusader drive for their second touchdown. The Notre Dame QB converted a two-point try to make the score 28–14. Too close for comfort with that potent offense.

On the next Saucon series, the Thatcher-Culver show flashed their late season form, skillfully moving the ball down field with a Thatcher twenty-five-yard first down, then a Culver thirty-five-yard first down. The next play saw Culver stopped short of a third first down by Crusader Nick Basenese at the Notre Dame 5 yard line. On the next play Culver plowed in from five yards out. Snead booted his fifth point after touchdown and the Panthers felt good about themselves, with eleven minutes and two seconds left in the game. Notre Dame was falling way short of expectations with their defense faltering badly. The previous Panther drive had only taken a mere minute and twelve seconds off the clock. The celebration grew in strength as it looked like we would win this one walking away.

Remember Tre Jordan? Notre Dame started their next series at their own 35 yard line. Reeling off six plays in a minute and forty-five seconds, Jordan scored his second touchdown. The Crusaders missed the extra-point kick but had closed the gap to fifteen points with nine minutes and seventeen seconds remaining in the game. It looked like the offensive fireworks might be heating up.

Saucon Valley went three and out in their next series as the Notre Dame defense, spurred on by their quarterback, finally showed up. Uh-oh! After a Kane punt from his own 18 yard line, the Crusaders started in great midfield position. As all great players do, Jordan put the team on his back, rushing and passing for positive yardage. Crafting a ten-play drive, he scored again on a seven-yard keeper. For the extra point, he found his receiver on a short out route, picking up the two-point conversion to put the visitors within striking distance. With four minutes and eight seconds left to play, Saucon Valley was within one score of seeing this game tied up. What had just happened? Saucon faithful didn't lose hope but were bewildered and concerned.

Brett Nesfeder sent the next kickoff into the end zone for a touchback, so the Panther's new line of scrimmage started at their own 20 yard line. Saucon could not convert, again going three and out to give the ball back to Notre Dame at midfield. Seven plays later, with almost three minutes remaining in the contest, Jordan found the end zone on a nine-yard scramble. Notre Dame opted to kick the extra point and locked the game in at 35 apiece with a minute and four seconds left on the clock. Twenty-one unanswered points in the fourth quarter had the Panthers on their heels! This game had finally lived up to all the pregame hype.

Wow, just wow. How quickly the momentum changes.

Coach Chromczak said he was thinking, *"Don't do anything stupid. Don't give the ball back to them. Ball control. Play for the tie. Then win it in overtime.* Phil was in the box, and I was standing next to Matt." Evancho surveyed his team as they trekked off the field, the scoreboard a bleak reminder of the dwindling time. "Fifty seconds left," he boomed with a resolute voice. "This," pointing to the scoreboard, "is exactly what we trained for." Continuing with a spark in his eyes he said, "We're going to get the ball, and we're going to return it to a good field position. We'll move it down the field, score, and win the game—because that's what we came here to do!" Coach felt if he was positive, lo and behold, they might forget the negatives, get focused on doing exactly what they needed to do, and turn this momentum around.

With this shootout tied, Nesfeder kicked off deep to the Saucon 8 yard line. Harka caught the ball and returned it seventeen yards to the home team 25 yard line. After not attempting a pass all night, Thatcher threw a play-action pass on first down to TE Kane. He was running full speed in the middle of the field and secured a huge thirty-yard gain. Austin Kaulius stopped him at the ND 46 yard line. Thatcher quickly lined up his team and spiked the ball to stop the clock.

Snead, standing on the sidelines was thinking he might have to kick his first field goal ever. Nervous feelings started to unsettle the young sophomore.

We hadn't punted the ball much all season, nor did we punt very well, so if we got stopped at midfield, we may be giving up poor field position to a dangerous foe.

Sitting or standing in the overcrowded press box, the noise was deafening. Gail would run outside the box, holler, and then come back in to resume her play-by-play announcing. We were so emotional about how the tide had turned in this game. The noisy crowd was standing as fans outside the box tried to raise the noise level higher.

We still talk about how emotionally exciting that was and how thrilling it was to be part of that, to sit up top and watch this exciting game unfold in the relative comfort of a warm press box heated by the body energy of everyone inside.

Down on the field, a calm Head Coach Evancho didn't see any panic in the players' eyes after we gave up the tying score. Some of the veteran players were ticked off at each other for letting the game slip away. But these Panthers had come to conquer.

Thatcher told *Morning Call* Reporter Tom Housenick, "I was thinking, *Are we going to pass the ball or run the ball and go into overtime?* I was glad the coaches gave me and my teammates a chance to win the game." With forty-six seconds on the game clock, Saucon came out on the next play in a gun trips right formation. With the top three Panther receivers split out to the right, Wolfe was the lone Panther on the left side, getting single coverage.

After the big gain to Kane, Thatcher saw a defensive formation he liked and zeroed in on an unlikely target—sophomore Alstan Wolfe. "There's a saying, 'When they're even, they're leavin',"

Thatcher said. "I saw them matched up one-on-one and wanted [Wolfe] to make a play." Thatcher was hoping to show his versatility after what Jordan had just done.

On the snap of the ball, Wolfe ran a deep-vertical streak route. Harka and Kemmerer ran other routes. Thatcher looked at them because Harka is the type of guy that always wanted the ball. But it just ended up going to Alstan. It wasn't predetermined. The QB saw a split-second opportunity with single coverage on Wolfe and heavier coverage on the others. With a quick fake to Culver, he let it fly high and long. "Prime Time Wolfe" leaped into the crisp night air and grabbed that perfect spiral at its highest point, snatching it away from the Crusader defender and landing on his feet. As the Notre Dame defender collapsed, Wolfe skipped and celebrated fifteen yards into the end zone with what has become known to locals as Alstan Wolfe after *The Catch*. Play of the game. Play of the entire year. Chris Michaels covered the play perfectly, remarking, "In about twenty-seven seconds, Saucon Valley regained the lead, 41–35. Who said they can't throw the football?"

The Catch, Photo credit: Vickie Wolfe

That broke the tie with thirty-seven seconds remaining. Mr. Perfection, Josh Snead, confidently hit the extra point for the Panthers to make the score 42–35.

Years later, Thatcher reminisced about his teammates. "Mike Kane and Alstan Wolfe, they were like some people where the game just comes naturally. Remember Alstan leaping up and ripping that ball off the guy's helmet? That wasn't just luck. Look at the way he could snatch a high pass with one hand, his balance never wavering. They were born athletes—Kane, Harka, and Alstan. Sure, we were all blessed with some incredible talent, but there's hard work too. Nobody slacked off, nobody took a play off. But Alstan, he earned that moment. Looking back, he was the perfect guy for that crazy play."

Wolfe was just a regular guy. He had been hoping for an opportunity to shine in this game. There's no denying that Alstan was a fantastic athlete. He just had it. As soon as that play was called, he knew in the back of his mind that he would get his shot because he was the isolated receiver to the near side of the field. Alstan said, "Whenever we run a vertical play, the first read is usually to the isolated receiver. If that's a good matchup, then the quarterback throws to that receiver. Me and Zach had connected really good in practice that week. During all the games leading up to Notre Dame, I had, like five catches that year. But yeah, this was just a great memory." Wolfe added, "After every game we went to Waffle House. Everyone just piled in at the Waffle House. It was like there was no room in there for any anybody else other than a football player. Yeah, I just remember getting the All Star Special. And then for me, personally, it was nice because I was only a sophomore with all these upperclassmen. I was pretty much a shy kid back then. I'd go to school, go to practice, go home, eat, sleep, repeat. I didn't really do too, too much. I had a core group of friends, and we'd play Madden together."

With no timeouts remaining and starting from their own 19 yard line after the Panther kickoff, Notre Dame's Jordan was sacked by Kane for a two-yard loss. That tackle would make Kane Saucon Valley's career sack leader.

With the clock winding down, Notre Dame tried a desperation "fumblerooski" play. Although breathtaking and entertaining, it kept the Saucon Valley fans anxious and on their feet. The play was eventually blown up by "Highlight Reel" Harka and stamped out by "King-Kong" Zrinski as time expired.

Tom Housenick writes:

> Mike Kane and Cody Zrinski made the game's final two tackles in what was the Colonial League's game of the year . . . What made the two Saucon Valley defenders overcome with excitement wasn't that the Panthers had knocked off the only other unbeaten—Notre Dame-Green Pond. It was because they were finally able to corral Jordan. He threw for 239 yards, ran for 113 yards and four scores, including three in the fourth quarter to help Notre Dame rally from a 21-point deficit. "Chasing [Jordan] around all night was not fun," Kane said. "A lot of plays in the second half were broken plays he made."
> It couldn't have been much fun defending the Panthers, either. Quarterback Zach Thatcher had 163 of the team's 391 rushing yards and scored three times."

Saucon Valley and Notre Dame had played a thrilling game and now only the Panthers remain perfect on the season. The final score of 42–35 kept their dream alive.

It was a fantastic night for the Panthers and a fantastic night for the Lower Saucon Valley-Hellertown communities. A record crowd of spectators and media were on hand to watch the Panthers make history and guarantee themselves at least a share of the 2015 Colonial League title.

Culver was his usual workhorse self, rushing twenty-four times for 201 yards while passing his predecessor, Savant, to become Saucon Valley's all-time leading rusher with 3,612 career yards.

Years later I watched the video of this game, listening to the announcers calling every play. Sitting on the edge of my seat throughout the entire broadcast, I got to relive it. Even though I had witnessed this game first-hand, recorded each play, and knew the outcome, I was absorbed in the moment. Like Yogi Berra said, "Déjà vu all over again!" It was truly one of the most exciting football games I've ever witnessed, and I somehow kept fairly correct stats.

Joleyce Adams, Culver's mom, told me:

> I'm a pretty reserved girl, but during this football season, there was no reservation in my screaming and yelling and jumping for him. I think it was like that for our whole family. It was just exciting to watch him display the talent he had. Everybody was hugging everybody at the end of that game. It didn't matter if you knew each other. Evan's stepdad and dad were hugging by the end of that game!
>
> I had my girls with me at the time. Couldn't sit in the stadium seats with the other parents. I had to move because my youngest child was still in the stroller. We would go in that little handicap spot where there's no seating. So I would go there because I couldn't sit, and I needed to stand and move around. I remember running when Evan ran. I'm running in the handicap section yelling and screaming "Go, go, go!" This guy in a wheelchair turned around and looked at me. He's like, "Are you okay lady? Is there something wrong with you?" Because I was screaming and running back and forth in the little area. He didn't know I was Evan's mom. I guess everyone [on the team] looked up to where I was at one point in the game, and I had my head down on the pole because I was freaking out. And he saw me freaking out. He wasn't

freaking out. But I was. And at the end of the game out of everybody freaking going crazy, he came to find me. He gave me the biggest bear hug you could possibly imagine!

With a record-setting crowd in the stands and noise levels higher than ever, Ryan Meyers remarked, "That's when we really felt like we had the town behind us."

Carvis calls this game as his best high school memory.

I would imagine a lot of people agree that was their favorite, favorite moment. It was our Senior Night. It was certainly a fun memory of mine. And I think the interesting part of it is a lot of people would say our senior class was a core unit with that team, but you must know that the junior class, a year behind us, made us who we were. I kind of found it ironic that the hero in that game was Alstan Wolfe making that catch at the end of the game. It ultimately gave us a chance at winning in the final seconds, because we had, for all intents and purposes, kind of pissed it away in that second half. As the game went on there were a lot of guys on the team that were unhappy with the way our second half played out. But I just think there was poetic justice, if you will, with Alstan being the hero in all of that, scoring the final touchdown.

Winners find a way to win, and even with the ugly games, Saucon Valley figured out a way to win.

For Karen Kane, the last home game was pure magic. "It was like something out of a movie!" she exclaimed, her voice still buzzing with excitement. The crowd crackled with energy and after the final whistle, she couldn't resist joining the joyous eruption onto the field. It was Senior Night, a night etched in everyone's memory, but for Karen, it went beyond Alstan's incredible catch. "It was a true team effort," she emphasized. "The coaches had to dig deep and refocus the players late in the game, just like they did against Southern Lehigh in the second half. There was a moment," she recalled, her eyes twinkling, "when one of the players shouted, 'We are not going into overtime. We're getting this job done!' And you know what? They did!"

Post game quotes:
Thatcher: "It wasn't just me; it wasn't just Evan, it wasn't just Alstan. Every single player contributed to this win, and I couldn't be prouder of them."

Kane: "I remember I just started screaming and then I laid down on the ground."

Carvis: "It showed our youth for a second. It helped us grow. We kind of needed that, for them to punch us in the face. We realized we were beatable and that was a wakeup call."

Culver: "It was absolute madness. I've never experienced anything like that in my life. That's something that will stick with this program and with all of us for the rest of our lives. It was something special for sure."

* * *

ND-GP would be our fourth opponent to head into the playoffs that year, finishing with a League record of 9–1 and an overall record of 11–2. After winning their District XI AA title, they would lose to Dunmore in the state regional playoffs. This was a record-breaking year for ND-GP and their best season since 2003.

Both Notre Dame-Green Pond and Northwestern were the only two Colonial League opponents coming within one score of upsetting Saucon Valley.

CHAPTER 15

BICENTENNIAL CUP

Some of these guys were playing in pain late in the season. There was no way they were going to let down one of their brothers and not play. So it was just a camaraderie and they were like brothers.
—*Kerry Kemmerer, Saucon Valley equipment manager and father of Kory Kemmerer*

THERE WERE SCENARIOS in which the Panthers might fail to reach the four-team AAA playoff bracket at 9–1, so they faced a must-win scenario at Palisades. Notre Dame-GP (8–1) was already the AA top seed with their next win over Wilson (1–8). They were on their way.

The Palisades Pirates represented the Colonial League's last-gasp chance to derail Saucon Valley. Beating the 5–4 Pirates would not appear to be a walk in the park, so the Panthers needed to be ready for an upset-minded rival. After all, the annual Bicentennial Cup, a year-end contest between these two schools, was also at stake. At the very least, with this win, the Pirates figured they could take that Cup away from Saucon Valley. Evancho needed to keep his team focused on the challenge immediately in their path, for a better chance at seeding in the playoffs or returning to the Eastern Conference tournament.

A loss to Palisades would not only blemish a perfect regular season record, but it would also force the Panthers into a shared title with Notre Dame-GP.

So with at least a Colonial League title-tie assured, the whole season came down to this one final rivalry game. The Bicentennial Cup and the Colonial League Title would both be secured with this one win. Saucon Valley had been challenged by Northwestern Lehigh, who was the last Colonial League school to have beaten them, now more than fourteen months before. They had been challenged by Southern Lehigh in an intense backyard rivalry. They had been challenged by the star-studded offensive powerhouse from Notre Dame-Green Pond. All three of those opposing teams would go on to play in the post season. But tonight's focus had to be fixed on the Pirates, who were seeking to tame this Panther.

Our Hogs had led the way all season, meeting every challenge and taking care of business. Never resting on their laurels, they prepared for this game like every other one before.

Now, captains courageous Thatcher, Culver, Kane, and Carvis needed to take their Panthers down to Palisades and dispatch their lone remaining hurdle before securing season goal number one. Anything could happen on any given night in the Colonial League.

Challenged by some of the hurdles they had to overcome to get here, they stepped back into their workmanlike mode in week ten practices.

Game Time

The Panthers quickly pounced on the Pirates, tossing them down to Davy Jone's Locker with a 49–7 victory and earning an outright, undefeated Colonial League Championship for the first time in a decade. There was now no question that the team from Saucon Valley was back!

By winning their game against Palisades, Saucon Valley had also retained the Bicentennial Cup, an award contested by the two schools as their annual end-of-year rivalry.

But Goal number one had been achieved—they'd won the Colonial League.

* * *

The Pirates lost their playoff matchup, closing out their record at 5–6.

Colonial League Champs
Photo credit Keith Riefenstahl, *Saucon Source*

CHAPTER 16

SEASON-ENDING MUSINGS

The Panthers—a comeback story?
—Chris Michael, RCN sportscaster

Game of the Year 2015
Photo credit Keith Riefenstahl, Saucon Source

BEST COMEBACKS

Game film and videos of opposing teams are an essential tool in a coach's toolkit and Colonial League representatives supported Saucon Valley throughout the season. As Bob Frey said, "People offered game films on opponents. Teams generally supported each other during a postseason run, and that helps make us a very close-knit group for the most-part."

As reported by Chris Michael of RCN's *Sportstalk* in November

2015, after this football team had wrapped up the regular season, there was plenty of exciting football news ahead.

> The Panthers—a comeback story? Didn't they win the Colonial League last year and get to the District Championship game? Yes, they did, but they wanted more. Not only did they want to avenge last year's painful loss to Bethlehem Catholic, but they went about their goals with a very workmanlike approach. They also kept their focus—something often lost among the modern-day athletes. They didn't hang their heads and sulk about how last season ended, but they sought out a higher set of goals—and achieved them.

Photo credit: Bob Frey

The Panthers would now face their old nemesis, Bethlehem Catholic (BECA), in a dreaded Saturday afternoon game at the District XI Tournament. This play-in game would be held at Liberty High School, BECA's home field. BECA had had Saucon's number historically and the winner would move on to the District XI Championship Game against the winner of the Lehighton and Blue Mountain game.

From Tiny Champs to High School Heroes

Mike Kane's football journey began, as it did for many of these team mates, as an 80-pound sprout. It was more than just a game; it was a shared experience that blossomed into a championship legacy. Karen Kane kept records of their victories over the years; 85-pound champions in 2006, conquering the 125-pound Suburban League in 2010, and remaining undefeated in middle school in 2011.

Karen vividly recalls a conversation with Barb Thatcher, Zach's mom, a shared premonition as they watched their young boys from the stadium seats. "Before we know it," we mused, "they'll be here every Friday night." Time truly does fly.

As high schoolers, the Eastern Conference title in 2013, co-championship of the Colonial League in 2014 and the 2015 League Championship Title, were three more awards to add to their portfolio.

Watching them grow up together on the field was a privilege. There was Zach, the quarterback, connecting with Michael—a connection that would carry on into high school. Every year, youth football culminated in a magical night under the Montford Illick Stadium lights.

There were heartbreaks too. The championship game against Parkland in the 125-pound division stands out. It was a close fight, a devastating loss that left some of the boys in tears. Yet, they played with tremendous heart. Fast forward to their senior year. Watching a re-run of one game on TV, she couldn't forget the announcer's words. He compared Saucon Valley to Parkland, pound for pound favoring our boys. Parkland had size on their side, a larger pool of players, but heart can't be measured in numbers.

Hellertown's Dimmick Park holds a treasure trove of memories. Coach Kim Brown instilled a culture of punctuality—"Fifteen minutes early or you're late!" he'd say. Under his guidance, practice times seemed to inch earlier each week, a testament to their burning desire to improve.

The camaraderie they shared at that young age was truly special. Football wasn't just a game; it was a passion that consumed them.

Even when they ventured into other sports—basketball for Michael, wrestling for some—football season brought them back together like a well-rehearsed play.

Karen goes on to say, "These boys are a remarkable bunch. Hearing them talk about their teammates, their lifelong friends, in these interviews warms my heart. It's a bond that transcends the gridiron, a testament to the power of youth football."

Coaching Impacts

Coach Phil Sams, the receivers and defensive backs coach, really stood out for Harka. There was a great sense of camaraderie between them. It wasn't just a coach-player relationship; more like a friendship. Coach Sams encouraged that sense of comfort with all his players. Maybe it had something to do with the fact that he also coached baseball, which some played too. Since he coached both receiver and defensive back positions, he fostered a very open and friendly environment, they never felt like they had to walk on eggshells around him.

PART III

CRUCIBLE OF THE PLAYOFFS

CHAPTER 17

DISTRICT XI PLAY-OFF GAME

We were pretty locked down the whole year. I mean, our defense was spectacular that year.
—Alstan Wolfe, Saucon Valley Panther (2014-2017)

JIM THATCHER, ZACH'S dad, had a preseason prediction which he shared.

I always knew this group of kids was special, even when they were young. You know, every youth league season they competed and won convincingly. So in looking back at that time, the youth league teams didn't play traditional Colonial League teams. We always competed against what would become these big and talented East Penn Conference players and we always held our own. I'll be honest with you, that group of kids did everything I predicted from when they were freshmen. The only thing I didn't have them down for was competing for the 2014 District XI title. That was the only year I got wrong. When PIAA realigned classifications there was always talk of certain schools having to disregard their size and play up to another level. We always knew Bethlehem Catholic was going to be there. There was no way getting around it. For Bethlehem Catholic, it all depends on who they recruit and bring onto their team. So in 2015, they had a good group of kids, including a couple of Saucon Valley kids our boys knew and were teammates with in youth football. But they transferred to the private school before the 2014 season. They were good in their own right.

Barb Thatcher, Zach's mom, chimed in, "My husband would always say it's too bad they went to BECA because our team could have possibly done even better."

Going into the 2015 postseason, what we had learned from Saucon Valley High School's fiercest opponents in the Colonial League was that the Panthers were winners. Notre Dame got chewed up by Saucon Valley's running game, but nearly pulled off their own undefeated season with a late-game tied score, before falling to the champs. Northwestern, Southern Lehigh, Salisbury, and Palisades had all entered the playoffs. In all, five Colonial League teams won ten games in the playoffs.

Three Hills To Climb—One Down, Two To Go
The Panthers knew their performance against BECA would be important for their future. They'd played well all year long but had never beaten BECA. BECA played in the big school East Penn Conference, so they were battle-tested every week against bigger, faster, tougher, and more skilled talent opponents.

There was a bit of another edge as well. The Panthers talked about some of those BECA players still living in Saucon Valley, as Jim and Barb Thatcher mentioned. They had opted to transfer to BECA when the Saucon Valley program was just starting to gel for a chance to play on a more established, successful football program. This was the place and the time for our homegrown talent of Saucon Valley School District to prove they were every bit as good as if not better than the private Catholic school recruits.

This BECA preseason review written by Greg Joyce for lehighvalleylive.com, gave us some insight into our next opponent.

The days when Bethlehem Catholic had losing seasons in football aren't too far in the past, but the way the last two years (2013–2015) have gone, they seem like distant memories. From 2010–12, the Golden Hawks were 6–24. Over the next two years, they captured district titles and won a total of 20 games. Bethlehem Catholic is in a strong position to continue that success under fifth-year head coach Joe Henrich. All-State dual-threat quarterback Julian Spigner returns for his senior year with a bevy of weapons around him, including receivers EJ Fineran, Nate Stewart and Nick Petros as well as a physical running back in Antwon Keenan.

The Golden Hawks' secondary could be one of the best in the area, with Fineran, Stewart and Joe Jay Smith along with Andre Blackett and Darius Aldridge in the mix. Bethlehem Catholic did lose three starters on the offensive line and while their replacements aren't as big, they may be a little more athletic, Henrich said. While last year's squad reached the state quarterfinals before bowing out to Somerset, this year's group has the potential to get there again with what they hope is a better ending. From senior wide receiver/defensive back EJ Fineran: "We're definitely riding that momentum into camp this year. We're trying to get on the same page we were last year. Our goal is to get as far, if not farther. We have the players to do it, we just gotta keep working hard."

From Head Coach Joe Henrich: "Sometimes you worry when you start winning, about getting into that comfort zone. We're not there at this point. We'll always continue to preach not getting into it. These kids are definitely hungry and eager to get back, if not further than what we did last year."

Both Spigner and Keenan were at the top of the District XI offense leader board when this game got underway.

BECA entered the tournament as the number two seed while Saucon Valley came in at number three. The previous year's game when they'd been soundly beaten by BECA in the District XI title game was very much on the minds and hearts of the smaller school Panthers.

Keith Riefenstahl said:

> Offensively, the Panthers average 47 points per game. Defensively, and in an arguably tougher league of AAAA schools, BECA only allows an average of 12. Evan Culver and his 1,971 rushing yards along with Zach Thatcher and his 768 will be working to keep the chains moving against the Hawks. Culver, Thatcher, and the Hogs (Steven Good, Christian Carvis, Ryan Meyers, Trey Polak, and Cody Zrinski) face their most competitive opponent of the year. The bigger Hawks run a 3-3-5 defense and are fast. They play physical and are good tacklers. Ralphy Lozada, a junior, is one of those tough tacklers. At five feet, eleven inches and 195 pounds, Coach Evancho points him out as a real good linebacker who plays right in the middle of the Hawks defense. The Panther coach is also impressed with senior defensive back Joe Smith. Smith is listed at a rangy six feet, three inches and 206 pounds. A ball-hawk, he is a Division I recruit.

BECA was very similar to Notre Dame. They ran a spread offense from the shotgun. They had a quarterback in Julian Spigner (Division I at Lafayette College) who could throw and run. Spigner was listed at six feet, three inches and 195 pounds. He had thrown for over 1,500 yards that season and had rushed for 679. He was one of the better dual threats in the Valley. If the ball was not in

Spigner's hands then it was likely being handled by Antwon Keenan (Division I prospect at Penn State). Like Culver (Division II prospect at Kutztown), Keenan averaged ten yards per carry. Rushing for 1,247 yards, Keenan stood at a solid five feet, eleven inches and 205 pounds and was second in the Lehigh Valley in touchdowns scored with thirty-two, just one behind Culver's thirty-three. BECA's leading receiver was Nate Stewart (Division I prospect at Montana State University). Stewart stood six feet two inches tall and 195 pounds and had twenty-five receptions for 571 yards. He also had two punt returns for touchdowns to his credit. Saucon had its own Division I prospect in Mike Kane (Colgate) and four who played their post high school football at Kutztown University (Nate Harka, Evan Culver, Alstan Wolfe, and Ryan Meyers).

BECA brought a potent offense to the field, averaging forty-four points per game with an arsenal of weapons that struck quickly. Their versatility on the ground and through the air, coupled with a dangerous special teams unit, made them a multidimensional threat.

The smart money went for BECA winning in another high scoring affair. Both defenses were squeaky tight, so this would definitely be anyone's game.

The advantage rested with (BECA), the parochial school team that recruited talented players throughout the Lehigh Valley. Saucon Valley had to rely on their homegrown talent. Both coaches had supreme confidence in their players.

This was a great game between two very talented teams who had met before at this level. It was the second Saturday game of the year for Saucon. The stadium at Liberty High School presented a big-school feel with its stadium-like seating on both sides of the field encased in the familiar rock-quarry stone found in other high-end school stadiums.

Played in one of Pennsylvania's largest high school stadiums, with seating capacity of up to fourteen thousand in addition to the standing room section. It was the home stadium for three large Bethlehem-area Eastern Pennsylvania Conference high schools. Liberty and Freedom shared their home field here along with Bethlehem Catholic High School. All three schools had sent their share of graduates to play college ball at all levels. The stadium, which was built in 1939 by Bethlehem Steel, had been described as a local football mecca.

The sentiment shared by many Saucon Valley fans at the game was that they had noticed when walking into Liberty when they played BECA, that Saucon Valley fans all sat together on our side of the stadium. Looking at BECA fans across the field, they sat separately from each other. There was much more of a sense of community on the SV side.

Still the best family entertainment in the area, advance tickets went for six dollars for adults and three dollars for seniors and students.

Family, community and brotherhood. There was a team of destiny on this field.

But which one?

It is very easy to argue that family, community and brotherhood are very powerful concepts all by themselves. But when those three come together along with determination and talent, incredible things are bound to happen.

Game Time

The 10–0 Panthers kicked off at Liberty High School in the first round of the District XI playoffs. The battles up front on the line of scrimmage defined the game. The Hogs earned an upper hand in the trenches and gave the Panthers good chances to keep their offensive machine rolling along. The white shirts (Saucon Valley) kept pushing and kept the brown (BECA) shirts from penetrating. Culver and Thatcher did what they do best and kept the drives alive. A steady diet of Culver and Thatcher led to a potent play-action attack by the Panthers.

Similar to the Notre Dame contest, this District XI play-off game started slow, with both teams trading their first two possessions.

Coach Chromczak shared his game plan:

> BECA was always a pretty good football team, and we didn't really look past that. I still think to this day in Lehigh Valley football that if you can win the district title, you'll do well in the state tournament. Football is so good here in the valley that you have a chance to go places against some of the best teams in other districts if you win here. I really think that we were just looking to get past BECA, but this game was obviously huge. The plan from the offensive side was to keep the ball away from Spigner. You do whatever you got to do. Don't turn the ball over and even if we're not scoring let's take time off the clock to keep the ball away from him. That's what we did. We ground out some yardage and defense played great. That was good football. I think the wind was blowing about thirty to forty miles an hour that day.

With that kind of wind in an open stadium, throwing quarterbacks can't be as accurate as they'd wish.

After feeling each other out, on second down and eight yards to go in Saucon Valley's third possession, the Panthers broke their huddle into an Ace shotgun spread formation with a single tight end and flanker on the right along with a "twins" look wide to the left. Culver was in the backfield to Thatcher's left. Thatcher squatted down into his familiar quarterback stance behind center and called the cadence, looked over the defensive line, took the snap, and handed off to Culver. Kane came in from his tight end position to block down and wall off the interior of the BECA defense. Both Panther guards, Carvis and Meyers, pull to their right, leading Culver around the right end. Harka ran in from his flanker position to stalk and seal his defender to the inside while the Hogs manned up on their assignments. Culver followed his Hogs and scampered forty-three yards untouched before cutting back to break a tackle and take advantage of Kemmerer's hustle-block on the last Hawk defender, allowing the scoring leader to add one more touchdown as he crossed the goal line with the game's first points. With his sixty-eight-yard race down the BECA sideline with just one minute and forty-three seconds remaining in the first quarter, BECA coaches, players and fans all got a close-up look at what "Silky Smooth" Culver and his Panthers could do.

This beautifully executed play along with Snead's spot-on kick were all the offensive points the Panthers would need this day, but it was still early in the game with three quarters yet to play and it was BECA's high octane turn with the ball.

So everyone got back to the business of why they were on that field.

The Hawks would answer late in the 2nd quarter with a nine-yard touchdown run by Antwon Keenan. Keenan's thirty-third touchdown of the season was set up with a fifty-yard reception on a fade route to BECA's Nate Stewart. BECA missed their extra point and the score stood at 7–6 with just over a minute to go until the halftime intermission.

As many spectators prematurely headed for the hot chocolate on this sunny but cold afternoon, Thatcher (wasn't he the quarterback?) took the ensuing kickoff at his own 13 yard line and slipped through a middle hole to return the ball sixty yards all the way down to the Hawk 27 yard line.

Running into a defensive wall, Thatcher kept his focus to make a great throw along the Panther sideline on fourth down and seven, spiraling the ball into Harka's sure hands to move the line of scrimmage down to the BECA 9 yard line and a Panther first down.

On the very next play, Thatcher rolled to his right and rifled a bullet to Wolfe in back of the BECA end zone with about ten seconds remaining in the fist half. Wolfe had slipped out of his cut but was agile enough to recover and make the catch above his head while on his knees. It was just another spectacular grab by the sophomore, another "day in school". Snead converted the final point of the game to put Saucon up 14–6 at the half.

The scoreless second half was filled with big plays but no scores.

Panther Defense Locked In
Photo credit: Keith Riefenstahl, *Saucon Source*

One of those plays included Culver putting himself in perfect defensive position to defend another deep pass to BECA's Stewart. The Hawks moved down field, deep in Saucon territory, threatening to add to their score. This time, Culver was able to see the ball and deflect it away in the Panther endzone on fourth down and five, forcing a costly BECA turnover on downs.

Another great play late in the third quarter came from BECA's Stewart returning a punt fifty-three yards and sending a shiver into the Panther faithful. We held our collective breath as it looked like he would break it open. But our Panther special teams closed the gap and put an end to that threat.

Three plays later Kane got in the way of a Spigner third-down pass, forcing BECA to punt again. No matter where Spigner looked, he had trouble connecting with his receivers thanks to the suffocating Saucon secondary.

The Saucon Valley offense deserves credit for gutting out a few timely fourth down conversions and flipping the field position at key times during the second half. Offensively, the Panthers kept the ball and the clock moving, as planned, to include a pair of eight-play drives in the fourth quarter.

But it was the Panther Hog defense that held a clinic, allowing BECA's Spigner only two yards rushing on eleven carries. He completed seven of his nineteen passes. The Panther "D" also held BECA's best running back and District XI rushing leader, Keenan, in check. Keenan was limited to eighty yards rushing on the day.

When asked about the Panther's gritty performance, defensive coordinator Chris Labatch said, "We saw a couple reads on film that we liked and we had the kids learn those reads. Our D-line owned the line of scrimmage. Our linebackers made the reads and filled fast. Everyone did their jobs and executed the game plan perfectly. I have to point out the play of everyone on the defensive line: Cody Zrinski, Trey Polak, Mike Kane, Ryan Meyers, Abe Lugo ,and Devin Van Vliet. They ate up blocks to let the guys behind them (Carvis, Kehs, and Paolini) fly around and make tackles."

It was a masterful game plan that limited Bethlehem Catholic's high-powered offense to 233 total yards of offense and only six points. The Hawks came into this showdown averaging forty-four points per game but were held to six. The Panthers, who boasted a stingy defense allowing merely fifteen points per game, won that contest by shutting down a superior East Penn Conference team.

Another payback game! Goal number two accomplished!

Asked what he said to his team after such a great victory, head coach Matt Evancho said, "I told them the same thing I tell them after every game: go and celebrate this win with your teammates, your family, and your fans, but when you wake up on Sunday, your minds must move on to our next opponent and winning a championship."

The season was over for all but three football powers from the Eastern Penn Conference (EPC) and Colonial League football programs. Parkland had won their AAAA contest as expected and Saucon Valley and Notre Dame-Green Pond were also still alive at this point.

Not many people outside the Hellertown-Lower Saucon community had given the 2015 Panthers much of a chance to take down Bethlehem Catholic, for all of the aforementioned reasons. Most sportswriters from the local newspapers circulated that opinion throughout the Lehigh Valley prior to Saturday's game. Reporters in the press box talked about how BECA, not Saucon Valley, would go on to the state playoffs. The experts in this instance, were wrong.

BECA was clearly supposed to win that game, but someone forgot to tell Saucon Valley! Not that the Panthers would have listened, because they BELIEVED in themselves. In the reality of the game, high octane offenses normally give way to dominant defenses.

With their families and community squarely behind them, this Panther band of brothers advanced to the District XI Finals against Lehighton High School.

These Saucon seniors were bright, articulate, and full of life. They were a lively bunch destined for success. The following Saturday, Coach Evancho, his coaching staff, athletic trainer, team captains, and all of the Panthers boarded the buses for their PIAA District XI championship showdown up north with the Lehighton Indians. The sun was still shining when they left their home stadium. It was dark before the first kickoff at 7 p.m.

Wolfe, who also played at Kutztown University after high school, gave some insight about the Panther secondary. "I was pretty much like a fill-in player. Whenever Culver needed a break. That was determined by the way he was running on offense, and he needed a break quite a bit. So I got to be on the field a good amount at corner. In the secondary, Thatcher was the captain, playing free safety. He made the defensive calls and told everybody where to be and what to look out for. He was such a good captain on both sides of the ball. Then, it was me, Culver, and Harka as a three-man rotation at corner."

CHAPTER 18

DISTRICT XI CHAMPIONSHIP

Their stadium was unlike anything I'd ever seen—super old-fashioned and intimate. Stands were packed right up against the field, creating a real bowl-like atmosphere.
—Nate Harka, Saucon Valley Panther (2012–2015)

RIEFENSTAHL ENCOURAGED THE faithful. "So load up the car or hop on the bus and be witness to another great night of Panther football. It's been a great ride so far and these Panthers will lay it all on the line to keep it rolling. Let's do what we can to help them out."

Saturday's high temperature was in the midforties and the low temperature Saturday night was in the low thirties. So this game came at a time for typical Pennsylvania late-fall—ear muffs, scarves, heavy jackets, and mittens weather, except for football coaches who wear shorts in November.

Things Worth Watching:
Going back to Riefenstahl's column in the *Saucon Source*.

Offensively, as they have done for much of this season in the Colonial League, the Panthers average 44 points per game. Lehighton only allows an average of 10 points per game in the Anthracite Football League. But we've faced this contrary point discrepancy before against Southern Lehigh, Northwestern Lehigh, Notre Dame and Bethlehem Catholic. Each time, HC Matt Evancho led his team to victory and a complete turnaround in those ratios.

Culver, Thatcher and the Hogs (Good, Carvis, Meyers, Polak and Zrinski) face another big challenge. The Indians have shown both a 5–2 and a 4–3 defense. They are not a big team, but they all play hard-nosed football and are all very good tacklers. Lehighton is led by senior linebackers Wyatt Clements (Division III prospect at East Stroudsburg) and Connor Frey. Clements is a stud, also looks the part at 6'1", 220, and hits like a linebacker when he finds the hole. He is fun to watch. According to Coach Evancho, Frey is also very good, coming in at 6'1", 210.

Culver has proven through the past 11 weeks that he does not need much room for his hips and feet to get moving. His 34 touchdowns and an average of 193 yards per game speak for itself. His per-game yardage would likely be north of 250 if he didn't spend a collective 84+ minutes off the field as a result of the Panthers saving him during Saucon Valley blowouts.

The Indians could pack the box and slow down Culver, then go after Thatcher. Thatcher was responsible for 1,800 dual-threat yards. He also could have easily posted more than two thousand yards if the coaches had kept him on the field during those blowout wins. His receiving trio of Harka, Kane, and Wolfe all averaged in the neighborhood of twenty yards per catch. Let's also not forget about Panther fullback Mike Paolini. "Big Mike" averaged seven yards per carry and had a knack for making the most of his runs when he wasn't blocking for the others.

Lehighton looked very similar to the Panthers in their offensive philosophy. They ran the ball, taking advantage of Wyatt Clements. Clements was a raging bull who ran angry. For a big guy, he ran with a low shoulder pad level which made him difficult to tackle. The Panthers surely tightened their chin straps before they flew to the ball when Clements carried.

It's no surprise that Coach Evancho was most concerned about Lehighton's run game. "They run a nice zone-read behind a good offensive line," he said. "We will need to tackle well and get to the ball." Wrapping up Clements was definitely a big key to this game.

Lehighton complemented Clement's punishing ability with a little dual-threat of their own. Indian quarterback Tyler Cann may not have been quite as explosive as Thatcher, but he was not afraid to call his own number. Listed at five feet, ten inches and 175 pounds, he made good decisions and played with a swagger. Cann had shown the ability to throw as well. Usually, the big pass plays targeted Nick Chambers, who at six feet, three inches had proven the ability to get behind the defense for long touchdowns.

Coach Evancho cited three priorities in preparing for this game against the Indians. First he wanted, ". . . the focus to be on the process of getting better." If the players stayed the course, "The rest will take care of itself," he said. He also said, "The execution of the game plan with no mental mistakes. . ." was key. Against quality opponents in championship games, it often comes down to the winner being the team that makes the fewest mistakes. Finally, Coach added that, "playing and practicing with energy" was a goal. He explained that the Panther players needed to "enjoy the time they are having with their teammates. They have created something special and should not miss out on that."

Many would agree that what these Panthers had created was indeed very special and that it was more than just the players who were soaking it all in. It's safe to say that the 2015 Saucon Valley football team had sparked a spirit within our community that none of us chose to miss.

Friends, family members, merchants, and many others from all over the Lower Saucon Township and Hellertown had embraced this team, rallying behind those young men and channeling a tremendous amount of support their way on game day, between games, and in the parades to and from away games. The Panthers were the buzz of the town, and rightfully so. It was a special time in our community. Those boys had given us all a wonderful gift. It had been a long time since we'd experienced this exciting level of football and this degree of "Panther Pride."

Game Time

After the Panther defense stopped the Indians on the opening drive of the ball game, it took Culver only two touches to find the end zone. It was an incredible run that started as a toss-sweep to the right but ended with Culver cutting back hard to his left and racing the distance for the game's first score. It was the first of five touchdowns for Culver and the first of many toss-sweeps on the night. The Panther's sure-footed kicker, Josh Snead, added the extra point for an early 7–0 lead. Snead would end the night perfectly, converting all eight of his extra points.

The Panther defense prevented the Indians from converting on a fourth and one at midfield. Saucon's offense then forged an eight-play drive that ended with another toss-sweep to the right. This time Culver scored from eight yards out and Saucon Valley grabbed a two-touchdown lead.

The road team from Saucon Valley scored the first three times they had the ball. The home team Indians started their next possession at their own 31 yard line after the next kickoff. On first down, Lehighton tried a quick-screen-pass into the Panther secondary. Big Mike Paolini stepped in front of the Lehighton bubble screen near the Panthers bench, picked off the pass in full stride and ran untouched twenty-five yards for the score, his hair flowing in the wind. It was the senior linebacker's second interception of the season and his first career pick-six.

Early in the second quarter, the Panthers held a commanding 21–0 lead.

"We worked a lot on that formation in practice," Paolini said. "We were expecting bubbles and screens. I did what I was told to do and just jumped it."

"Mike made a fantastic play on the ball and the rest is history," Evancho added. "That was a big momentum change for us."

The Indians would get on the scoreboard late in the quarter courtesy of a twenty-seven-yard touchdown pass from quarterback Tyler Cann to wide receiver Tegan Durishin with just over four minutes remaining in the first half. Lehighton seemed to have stopped the bleeding and was attempting to make some headway in changing the pace of the game. However, the Panthers would have the last word as Coach Chromczak crafted a twelve-play drive to keep momentum on our side with a short touchdown plunge by Culver with thirty seconds left in the half. Culver's score was set up on the previous play by Thatcher's toss to Kane, taking the Panthers down to the Indians 2 yard line. Walking into the locker room with a halftime score of 28–7, we were feeling good.

The Panthers wasted little time adding more points in the third quarter with a three-play drive. Culver took the handoff, attacked the right side, and cut back hard to the left to find the end zone. It was his fourth TD of the night. The thirty-one-yard scamper with Snead's extra point extended the Panther lead to 35–7.

"We've tried to break him of that the last couple of weeks," Evancho said, "because of the way the other teams' linebackers flowed a little bit more. Lehighton's linebackers flowed over the top, so he was able to hit those cutbacks the way he has all year."

The Panther defense would again bend but not break, handing

the ball back to their offense. Field marshal Thatcher marched his team seven plays down field to finish with yet another toss-sweep to the right side for "Silky Smooth" Culver's fifth and final touchdown of the night. Culver's score and Snead's kick made it 42–7. Panther dominance on both sides of the ball in the second half put the mercy rule into effect. The thirty-five-point differential stood with four minutes and thirty seconds remaining in the third quarter. Mercy rule! In a District XI Championship game and against the home team!

Culver was given the rest of the night off, but he wouldn't warm the bench, preferring instead to transform himself into a cheerleader for his teammates.

Kehs and Steven Rose rushed for touchdowns in the fourth quarter to finish off a 397-yard effort on the ground by Saucon, while Wyatt Clements and Mike Mayernik would each score for the Indians.

Lehighton's Wyatt Clements didn't reach 100 yards (109 on twenty carries) until he scored against Saucon Valley's reserves with eight minutes and one second left in the game.

"We had opportunities early to keep drives going," McCarroll said, "and to score, but we made some mistakes that were uncharacteristic of us. All the credit goes to Saucon Valley."

At the final buzzer, Saucon Valley celebrated its second district championship with a resounding 56–20 Panther victory.

Following the Hogs and utilizing key blocks from Kane and Paolini, Saucon Valley tallied 440 yards of total offense while their defense limited a potent Indian attack to only 278. Many of those Clements rushing yards came in the waning minutes of the game against the Panther JV squad, who reaped valuable playoff experience. It was another impressive Panther performance on both sides of the ball. Saucon Valley claimed District gold.

As usual, Culver had a fantastic game. For the season he had 231 carries with 2,328 yards and thirty-nine touchdowns. Quarterback Thatcher had a quietly productive night and now had 1,014 passing yards to his credit for the season, making it his second season in a row eclipsing the one-thousand-yard passing mark. He also had a very respectable 890 yards rushing.

When offensive linemen Polak, Zrinski, Good, Carvis, and Meyers came off the field after a Saucon Valley touchdown, Culver was the first one to greet them, even though he hadn't scored that particular touchdown. The senior running back's night was done by that point, but he wanted to show his appreciation for the guys in the trenches who blocked for their teammates.

"He'll be the first to tell you how proud he is of the offensive line, the receivers, and running backs who block for him," Head Coach Matt Evancho said. "He gets all the glory but gives credit to them every day."

Lehighton coach Tom McCarroll said Saucon Valley had a lot of weapons and balance, but Culver was the best back his club has seen this season. "Hands down," he said. "He's a 2,000-yard back. There aren't too many around here. He's a special player."

That credit, Culver said, went to all the Panthers who made it possible for the program's first 12–0 season. "The line did an outstanding job," Culver said. "I can't describe all the work they did. It's a great group to run behind." If you asked those linemen, they'd say they had a great running back to finish what they started.

"This was our goal, starting after the loss last year to BECA," Culver said. "We wanted to get back to the same spot. We knew the [district title] wasn't going to be handed to us. It was something we worked hard for all year. There were no distractions."

Mission Accomplished

This was the biggest goal from the outset of the year. Win the Colonial League, beat BECA and win the District XI title. Mission accomplished. What would be next?

Lehighton was now in the rearview mirror and the 2015 District XI Championship forever a sweet memory for the Evancho Heartbeats and Harmonies Football Traveling Show. The Panthers now needed to direct their focus even farther north to perennial playoff team Scranton Prep.

It was time to get ready for the first round of the PIAA State Tournament.

Could we do this? It was new territory for this small-town school from Hellertown and Saucon Valley. Originally they thought that district championship would be the high point—the storybook ending of beating Bethlehem Catholic in the District Championship game and coming full circle.

But from this point forward Saucon Valley was heading to states, navigating uncharted waters because they hadn't thought that far. Had anyone really conceptualized what it meant to win the district title? Perhaps not. From this point forward, they would build on an already successful season, one that was planned from the beginning. We were heading to Scranton! We had been up there two years prior for the Eastern Conference Championship. So a few of the coaches and players were familiar with playing football in coal country.

District Champs, Photo credit: Keith Riefenstahl

Ryan Meyers was pretty happy with the next matchup, saying, "... it was nice to have two teams from the Valley advancing into the state playoffs. When we beat teams, we tended to gained their fans a little bit. Then as the season progressed, it felt like we had the whole District XI fan base behind us."

Scranton Prep had been a 37–7 winner over another perennial playoff team, Berwick, in the District II final, setting up the next game to be a regional semifinal thriller set for the day after Thanksgiving— "Black Friday."

CHAPTER 19

REGIONAL SEMIS

Why can't it be us? Why can't we be in the state [finals]?
—Ed Chromczak, Saucon Valley offensive coordinator

LOOKING OVER THE film on Scranton Prep, the coaching staff saw opportunities where the team could take advantage. Their starting running back was banged up. So we knew their running game was going to struggle a bit. We had to go up there to play at Valley View's Veterans Memorial Stadium, which was five miles from Scranton Prep High School. So it was basically a home game for them. But at that time, we thought why not us?

As they had been doing every week since July, the team prepared and practiced for the next game, even though it was Thanksgiving week. The oddities here were interesting. Saucon Valley would play their first ever football game after Thanksgiving Day. So while the moms and dads prepared for their own traditional family festivities around a big holiday meal, the coaches and players focused on their next game to be played on Black Friday.

Thanksgiving Day, a time when most of America prepares the big family meal, watches the parades, catches some professional or college football, and enjoys family time, practice for this veteran team continued unabated. So while fans of the Easton-Philipsburg high school teams headed out to watch their annual Turkey Day rivalry, the Saucon Valley moms prepared and served a team breakfast before heading home to take care of their other Thanksgiving Day activities. It should be noted that everyone took some time off. Coach Sams, as an alumnus of Easton High School, went to that game with his son after practice concluded. Coach Evancho, also an Easton alum, went to the game to watch his daughter cheer on his alma mater.

Some of the Thursday dinner crew who had prepared and served the pregame meals to the team every week all year took part in this effort and enjoyed it. Karen Kane, Barb Thatcher, Kim Kemmerer, Brenda Carvis, and others all took part, helping with the food prep. The boys were all very appreciative. "I talked to about a dozen of the players, and I was amazed at how much maturity I saw in those boys," recalled Joleyce Adams. "Between the parents and the coaches, they all did such a wonderful job in raising those guys."

Small Town Big Dreams
Photo credit: Keith Riefenstahl, *Saucon Source*

One of Coach Evancho's favorite memories from that 2015 season was Thanksgiving Day. The mothers did it all, a fascinating statement from somebody who lives and breathes football and at that time was preparing his team for the biggest game of their lives.

The morning began with his team on the field, walking through their drills, putting in the extra work, running plays, keeping focused. Their efforts were soon rewarded as the sight of their moms appearing with breakfast. It was a heartwarming moment that still stays with them. "It was more than just a meal," he reflected. "Seeing the kids gather around the table, united by their love for the game—and appreciation for their parents' support—that was truly special."

Not one kid was late for practice that day. They knew how important this practice was. They knew that what they were doing was different. They knew that once they got through that first round, they could do something distinctly special. Something really big could happen as long as they kept their focus. That took on a different perspective. They felt what they had done in the regular season was impressive, but in the grand scheme of things, there were very few high school teams still playing at that time of the year. And this time we were one of them. Coach remembers going up into the stands and taking a picture of the team warming up—a special moment he'll never forget. Watching them in their element, enjoying each other, going through their drills, practicing, preparing, getting ready, bonding. Mom Karen Kane recalled thinking, after the Lehighton win and realizing the last practice the next week was on Thanksgiving Day, "We have to feed them. We can't not feed them. But we didn't want to jinx anything, so we approached Coach Evancho and said we're going to bring in breakfast. So we brought in bagels and cream cheese, smoothies, chocolate milk, and orange juice." So that was Thanksgiving morning. Nobody complained about it. They were a special group of guys, and they were accomplishing something that no other Saucon Valley football team had done in history.

Praise for these boys comes from all corners, but at this time, Coach Chromczak weighs in. "I've been coaching for almost thirty-some-years now, and it was the best team I've ever been around. Great kids, great young men who loved to be around each other.

I can still remember practice on Thanksgiving morning. We're all laughing and having a good time. Seriously, they just loved being around each other. We got breakfast too! I think Goodie's dad made milkshakes for everyone."

On Black Friday, the seven o'clock kickoff at Valley View (Veterans Memorial) Football Stadium in Peckville, PA, brought a crazy week to a climax. Determined, these Panthers did their best to make it another magical night. They saw the opportunities. They saw their own destiny. They sensed what could be accomplished. They didn't lose sight of the fact that they were facing another playoff contender who could get the upper hand and steal this moment away.

Just walking off the bus up in the Poconos, into the cold, dark night air, it felt like the perfect night. The weather was crisp out. It was not warm, but not too cold. Thatcher, walking off the bus, said he thought confidently, *Oh, this is gonna be okay.*

Peckville is in northeast Pennsylvania, a region brimming with natural beauty, historical significance, and cultural charm. Archbald Pothole State Park is to the north. Clarks Summit to the west, Scranton to the south and Lake Wallenpaupack farther to the east. It boasts a strong and dedicated high school football fanbase where local communities rally behind their teams and create an exciting atmosphere at games. Scranton Prep was a consistent powerhouse with a strong winning tradition. Community pride was solidly behind their football team. We'd be playing in their backyard.

Hometown family, friends, students and fans travelled those seventy-seven miles in the dark for one more chance to watch their boys get after it with the best District II had to offer.

PIAA Quarterfinals, Photo credit: Keith Riefenstahl, *Saucon Source*

Panthers Enter Regional Play

District XI Champion Saucon Valley Panthers took the field at Memorial Stadium in Peckville against the District II Champion Scranton Prep Cavaliers in the first round of the PIAA State Tournament. Out of the Lackawanna Conference, Scranton Prep posted an 11–1 record. This game was weird, with no bands in attendance. Their school didn't have one. Ours was off to Florida for a long-planned trip to a Disney band competition, but we overcame their absence with noise of our own! The Jungle had traveled with us. The community had come along, not wanting to miss this game.

Offensively, the Panthers now averaged forty-five points per game while Prep's defense conceded only seven. Where had we seen this disparity before? It comes up like a psychological gauntlet of its own in every game.

The Cavaliers ran a base 4-4 defense and did a great job of getting good angles flying to the ball. Scranton Prep may have been the biggest team Saucon had yet faced this year. The Cavaliers were led by six foot, four inch Corey Christian, who at 270 pounds, bench-pressed

335 and squats 425. He had a vertical jump of 33.5 inches. He was one of their team leaders and was recruited to play at the Division II University of Albany. Thor Balavage (Division III Newman College) weighed in at six feet, two inches and 270 pounds and was also a team leader. Both were seniors and played defensive end.

The Hogs would be challenged to establish themselves in the trenches against the bigger Prep defensive line. Both Carvis and Good at 185 pounds gave up some significant weight inside, but intangibles like intelligence, intensity, and toughness were often determining factors in football match-ups. We were counting on our guys to have the edge and continue playing smart.

The Cavaliers, like so many other teams, game-planned to stop the Panther rushing attack.

This team had won their 2015 District II Class AAA title, and they ultimately repeated in 2016, 2017, and 2018. So they were no slouch.

Prep, wearing their yellow and purple, deployed an offensive play selection looking very similar to the Panthers. Their average of twenty-nine points per game and preference to run the ball took advantage of an offensive line that hulked out at an average of 245 pounds per man. Their featured back was junior Ricky Morgan, who measured five feet, eleven inches and weighed 170 pounds. He was not very big, but he was quick and shifty. Morgan hiding behind the big Cavalier line could be problematic for the Panther "D." For the most part, the Cavaliers liked to come right at you with in-your-face smash-mouth football. Running some Full House and Double Tight looks to go along with their base Twins set, Prep tried to toss out to the perimeter and outflank the Panthers, allowing Morgan to get the edge and make the turn up field.

It had been a great ride so far. These Panthers had put their heart and soul into each game, leaving it all on the field. This game was sure to be no different.

Game Time

The Cavs also ran Power off tackle and tried to trap the center of the Saucon Valley defense with their fullback Tyler Stafursky. Stafursky rumbled at six feet, two inches and 230 pounds. The Panthers played smart, trusted each other, and pushed off their blocks to contain the Prep rushing attack. Prep mixed in some spread looks and had a decent passing attack. In addition, the Cavaliers used a little creative trickery in their game plan. The Panthers played a rugged, disciplined style of ball to get their share of defensive stops.

The first half lived up to the billing. Trench warfare, ground-and-pound runners, and passing-receiving brilliance gave the fans of each team reason to believe.

Saucon Valley got off to a great start playing "bend but don't break" defense, jumping on top 14–0. Saucon's first score came courtesy of a three-play drive with Thatcher keeping the ball on an option and scampering twenty-six yards to pay dirt. The second touchdown resulted from a Cavalier fumble caused by Kane and recovered by Meyers. On the very next play, Culver burst through the Cavalier defense for a fifty-five-yard touchdown run.

Scranton Prep answered with a pair of their own touchdowns by quarterback Kevin Holmes. The first was a three-yard touchdown pass that capped a methodical sixty-three-yard drive. The second, a thirty-yard play-action bootleg pass found Wes Simons behind the Panther defense. Uh-oh!

On our next series, a chop block penalty in the second quarter forced Saucon to punt. A clip nearly derailed the next series before the Thatcher-to-Kane connection saved momentum and led to a back-breaking score against Prep before halftime.

Saucon Valley regained possession with three minutes and twenty seconds remaining in the half and reclaimed the lead. That drive was highlighted by a twenty-yard quarterback draw by Thatcher, along with a pair of passes to Kane. The first was a thirty-yard completion over the middle down to the Cavalier 17 yard line. The second saw Thatcher escaping out of the pocket, scrambling toward the goal line when he saw Kane open in the end zone. Kane had to dive into a low throw, roll over, and bounce up on his feet to reveal a good catch in the end zone for a twelve-yard touchdown reception. Snead made his third extra point to put the Panthers up 21–14 at the half.

The Panthers received the second half kickoff and wasted no time getting back to business. On the very first offensive play, tailback Culver caught a quick toss right pass and sped sixty-two yards for another Panther touchdown. Snead again did his thing to extend the Saucon lead by two scores to 28–14.

Panther defense then forced a three and out, which was bad news for Prep, because Culver would get the very next hand-off and speed off for another sixty-yard touchdown dash. Culver's highlight reel run and Snead's point after made the score 35–14 with nine minutes and seventeen seconds left in the third quarter. Panthers were feeling a win.

On the next series, Saucon's defense forced a Cavalier punt, and the Panthers forged another nice drive. Scranton Prep, however, would take advantage of a fumble, converting it to points with a sixty-five-yard wheel-route touchdown play. Prep's David Horvath raced out of the backfield and up the sideline to snag a deep throw by Holmes and finished for the touchdown. The Cavaliers missed their extra point, keeping the score at 35–20 with just under a minute remaining in the third quarter.

A Panther personal foul gave the Cavaliers life midway through the fourth quarter.

However, any hopes of Prep making a comeback were snuffed out when Culver, now stalking the secondary as a cornerback, intercepted Holmes in the end zone with about three minutes left in the game. "That felt good," Culver said. "I knew what that meant for us." The Panthers would keep the ball on the ground and run the clock down. Despite a holding call and a personal foul that negated two lengthy Culver runs on the ensuing drive, and much to our delight, Thatcher scored on a busted play! All the Panthers went right, but Thatcher wisely went left for a twenty-two-yard touchdown run with thirty-six seconds remaining in the game. Snead connected for his sixth extra point of the night to close out another brilliant 42–20 Panther road victory.

Culver again headlined the effort, gaining a spectacular 346 yards on eighteen carries and three touchdowns. He averaged nineteen yards per carry and now had forty-two touchdowns in the 2015 season. He turned big gains into touchdowns, scoring on runs of fifty-six, sixty-two, and sixty yards and the Panthers never trailed in a satisfying win at John Henzes-Veterans Memorial Stadium in Lackawanna County.

Thatcher's stat sheet was also impressive, rushing for 148 yards on twelve carries and completing two huge passes to Kane for a total of seventy-eight yards. Thatcher now had 1,038 rushing yards to go along with his 1,092 passing yards and was in the school thousand-yard record book for the second year in a row in both categories. Impressive dual-threat numbers coming out of our Panther backfield.

The Panther record improved to 13–0, keeping their season alive. They now advanced to the PIAA State Quarterfinals against District IV champion Selinsgrove at the Northern Lehigh stadium in Slatington the following Friday night. It would be closer to home in a stadium we were familiar with, but we'd still be the visiting team.

In the aftermath of it all, Head Coach Evancho was not happy with how some of his players had behaved on the field. Penalties had marred an otherwise spectacular night, with a total of nine for 118 yards. Not at all what we expected to see from that team. All but one of the penalties were of the double-digit variety. Despite enjoying a comfortable cushion, Coach Evancho lashed out at his players at halftime because of the actions a few had taken late in the second quarter. "Some of it I can't say, but the message was: that wasn't us in the first half," Evancho said. "That's not how we play. That wasn't how I coach them to play and it's not the way to act. I'm not happy with the way we lost a little poise, lost some character. We'll talk about that on Monday and get a clean game next week."

Kane added that there were two ways to look at the penalties the last couple of weeks. First, there was the angle as a player, who just did battle for forty-eight minutes to help take a program where no other Saucon Valley football team had been. "It's a good thing to have to yell at us," he said, "because I guess we care too much." Then, there was the mature recognition that there was no need to take it to the level of punishment—held by the officials and, eventually, the coaches. "The message [at halftime] was to keep calm, stop doing stupid stuff, stop yelling, and talking to the refs," he said. "That's not how to win games."

CHAPTER 20

CULVER RAN LIKE A MAN TONIGHT

I like to win too much.
—Bobby Bowden, College Football Hall of Fame Coach

EVERYONE WAS EITHER listening to music on their headphones, getting ready, getting pumped up, or just looking out the window enjoying the scenery. The coaches weren't walking up and down the aisle talking to players and trying to get them excited. The players weren't laughing but were pretty silent going to the games, getting their minds focused. Getting ready for the game. It was a business trip. On the way back, it was a different story. Those boys were boisterous, hooting and hollering, excited about extending the season and playing another game.

The 13–1 Selinsgrove Seals had defeated Greater Johnstown 49–28 to advance and face the Panthers in the state quarterfinals.

It was another fantastic week to be part of the Saucon Valley community. These Panthers worked hard, won some tough games, set new records almost every week, and moved beyond where any previous Saucon Valley or Hellertown High football team had ever gone.

They were only two wins away from a chance to play for a PIAA state title in Hershey.

But, first things first. The Panthers stuck to their weekly methodical routine, making all the necessary preparations just like they had for the past thirteen weeks. Come Friday, it was going to be time to once again unleash the Panther Beast!

> Snead's favorite moment of the season was leading into the Selinsgrove game. "That week of practice Coach had me working on pooch kicks, so I stood out on the game field for thirty or forty minutes setting up four cones and practicing pooch kickoff kicks. Then I got to attempt one in the Selinsgrove game, and they ended up fumbling it. I was relieved to see that payoff in a game. That was pretty big for me."

The Saucon Valley High School Band returned from their Florida trip and performed at the highly anticipated matchup.

This football team has already made history, advancing further in postseason play than any other football team in the history of the school. But that didn't mean it should end here. The Panthers wanted more, and they'd have the opportunity on Friday, December 4, when they faced off against the Selinsgrove Seals in the PIAA state football championship quarterfinal round in Slatington.

Excitement for this game had been building all across Lower Saucon Township and Hellertown since the Panthers had defeated Scranton Prep in the championship's first round. These Panthers and Parkland, the only other District XI team playing that weekend, carried the hopes of the Greater Lehigh Valley into the state tournament. Remember that earlier reference to these Panther players being pound for pound better than Parkland? You might also remember that an assistant coach at Parkland in 2015 was none other than Bret Comp, Matt Evancho's pal from Wilson Area, now coaching the wide receivers.

To reward residents for displays of Panther Pride, *Saucon Source* and Burke Insurance Agency sponsored a Facebook photo contest.

TV stations from Selinsgrove and the Lehigh Valley broadcast the quarterfinals. Service Electric broadcast the game live on its Channel 2 Sports channel and rebroadcasted it at 10 p.m. RCN broadcast the game at 9:30 p.m. on Channel 4 (Channel 1004 in high definition). Other local television stations, radio stations, and cable providers serving northeastern and central Pennsylvania also broadcast the game live or recorded for later airing.

The winner would advance to the state semifinals against the Academy Park-Imhotep Charter winner. A loss would end the storybook ride.

Offensively, the Panthers continued to average forty-five points per game and would look to feed Culver, who was running better than ever. But impressive numbers didn't only belong to him. Thatcher was also racking up the yards and touchdowns. This duo alone presented a challenge to any defense. And when they ran behind the Hogs (Good, Carvis, Meyers, Polak and Zrinski), opposing players found themselves backing up constantly.

Selinsgrove, however, would be up to the task. They were loaded with seniors and played hard, blue-collar football. The Seals ran a base 3-5-3 defense and had some size up front. Coach Evancho stressed, "We need to sustain blocks and be mentally prepared for multiple looks up front." The Hogs would need to be alert and execute their responsibilities against an aggressive Seal defense that showed an awful lot of movement. Culver didn't need much room to move, but the Seals didn't give much either. Culver, Thatcher, and the Hogs were facing another big challenge by this Seal defense. Senior fullback Mike Paolini would have a few opportunities out of the backfield to keep the chains moving for the Panthers.

Selinsgrove would pack the box with eight players using a lot of shifting and movement. They would try to smother the Panther rushing attack and force Saucon Valley to throw. The leading tackler for the Seals was inside linebacker Jack Gaugler (Division III Bloomsburg). He was a six-foot, 240-pound senior with 133 tackles and two sacks on the season. Gaugler and his seal pod were noticeably aggressive to the ball.

Selinsgrove also had an offensive dynamo in senior Running Back Juvon Batts (Hudson Valley Community College). He was five feet, eight inches tall and 185 pounds with great vision and a big-time burst. Batts in the open field could be a big problem for the Panthers. He had the potential to be a gamechanger. During the 2015 season Batts had already rushed for 1,785 yards and scored twenty-two touchdowns. Against Johnstown, Batts had proved to be the Seals' go-to guy as he carried an astonishing forty-three times for 276 yards and five touchdowns. Coach Evancho was impressed with Batts, saying, "We need to tackle really well and not let him get started." Batts was, no doubt, the Seals' primetime guy.

And the Seals weren't just one dimensional thanks to sophomore quarterback Logan Leiby (Division III Bloomsburg scholar athlete). Leiby was listed at six feet tall and 187 pounds and had thrown for an impressive 1,810 yards and twenty-two touchdowns. Leiby played with poise and had shown the ability to carve up a defense when he had time to throw. His preferred receivers were Colin Hoke (Division III Susquehanna Academic Honor Roll) and Nick Swineford. If it weren't for their jersey numbers they would be easily confused. Hoke was five feet, eleven inches and 185 pounds while Swineford checked in at six feet and 180 pounds. Both were seniors and both had close to six hundred yards receiving.

Selinsgrove was effective at mixing their runs and passes. Like Saucon, they ran out of the "I" formation, spread the defense out, and used the shotgun. They capably deployed drop-back and play-action passes from both schemes. The Seals also ran a very nice bootleg action series.

This weeks' opponent had their own version of the Hogs. Up

front were three seniors, a junior, and a sophomore, averaging 230 pounds across the offensive line. Those Seals were athletic and persistent. They did seem to struggle at picking up the blitz, though. Kane would try to get to Leiby before he could set his feet and throw. He could have a very big night coming off the edge to upset Leiby's rhythm.

So here we go again. The Friday Night Lights would be burning brightly for this PIAA Quarterfinal in Slatington. Saucon Valley was one of eight elite AAA football teams still playing in the state of Pennsylvania. Four of them would be finished for the season after that night. The Panthers were seeking perfection against the Seals. The emphasis on maintaining blocks and coverage assignments was vital. Turnovers, penalties, and mental mistakes often make the difference in championship games. Saucon Valley had played well the last week in spite of being penalized for over 100 yards. They'd also lost a fumble where they normally won the turnover battle.

As teams move deeper in the playoffs and face stiffer competition, mistakes become more costly. Each team was well-coached and had certainly addressed what they needed to do in order to continue their quest for the next title.

The preparation and practice was done. The time had come for the Panthers to once again focus their collective efforts, execute their assignments, and go all-in for forty-eight minutes. The time had come for the players, cheerleaders, student body, and band to board the busses and once again travel north. The time had come for the Hellertown and Lower Saucon community to stand firmly behind their Panthers and give them unwavering support. Coach Evancho called for a raucous "sea of red and black [in the stands]."

We delivered!

Friday night the Saucon Valley Panthers lost the coin toss and the Seals opted to defer their option to the second half.

So the Panthers received the opening kickoff and used just seven plays to march sixty-nine yards for their first touchdown of the night. The score came on a fourth and goal from the 3 yard line. Air Thatcher opened the assault by rolling to his left and rifling a pass to Harka, who made the touchdown grab with a Seal defender draped all over him. Snead converted the extra point to put Saucon up 7–0. We were off!

Saucon Valley scored again two plays later when Evan Culver intercepted Logan Leiby's pass and returned it twenty-eight yards for a pick-six. It was Selinsgrove's first offensive play of the game. Snead would again convert to put the Panthers up 14–0 with seven minutes and fifteen seconds remaining in the first quarter.

The teams traded punts with Selinsgrove gaining some offensive rhythm. The Seals were able to drive to the Saucon Valley 8 yard line, but the Panther defense had enough. On the next three plays, the Seals tried to run the ball and spring their stud, Juvon Batts. Panther defenders saw it coming and were all over him. On fourth and goal from the 4 yard line, the Seals tried to pass for a score. Defensive end Kane speed rushed from his position at the end of the line of scrimmage, flushing Leiby to his right toward the hospitable welcome and open arms of Meyers and Paolini. Leiby had no choice but to throw a prayer into the end zone that was spiked to the ground by Harka for an incomplete pass. The Seals took their best shot of the night and the Panther "D" held tight.

Not only did the defense stand firm, but on the subsequent series Thatcher marched the offense right back the other way. Saucon Valley put together a twelve-play drive that covered ninety-seven yards. Culver exploded up the middle from eight yards out, powering his way into the end zone with three minutes and fifty-two seconds left in the half. Snead kicked the final point of the half and Evancho's team walked into the locker room leading 21–0.

The Panthers got flagged with a fifteen-yard unsportsmanlike conduct penalty and were fortunate not to get another fifteen-yarder along with a possible player ejection.

It had only been one week earlier when Saucon racked up a

boatload of penalties late in a win over Scranton Prep. Evancho didn't want it to get any worse than it had in the second quarter against the Seals. "I told them it was up to them to take care of it in the second half," Evancho said, "and I think they responded well." Aside from that brief lack of discipline in the second quarter and a few physical mistakes, the Panthers controlled the Seals from the beginning.

The Panthers picked up where they left off to start the second half. Playing solid defense, limiting the Seals to an eight-play drive that ended in another punt, the Saucon Valley offense then came right back by uncorking a ninety-yard touchdown run by Culver. He must have run so fast that the cameraman missed the play! With eight minutes and fifty-two seconds remaining in the third quarter, Snead converted another extra point to put the Panthers up 28–0.

Selinsgrove returned the next kickoff to good field position. The defense bent but did not break, bringing pressure that forced Leiby to look for refuge rather than his downfield receivers. Threatening to score with a first and ten from the Panther 29 yard line, Leiby was forced to roll hard right by Zrinski pushing everyone out of the way. Big Mike Paolini, smelling blood in the water, attacked Leiby from his outside linebacker position. Running out of options, Leiby tried to force a pass that was intercepted by Wolfe.

It was another turnover that led to more Panther points. Saucon Valley marched sixty-seven yards in eight plays, with Culver powering his way in for a two-yard touchdown score. Snead successfully booted his fifth extra point of the night and with four minutes and twenty-nine seconds to play in the third quarter, the mercy rule kicked in with the Panthers working on a 35–0 shutout.

This was Saucon Valley's second mercy-rule game in the playoffs—clearly a powerhouse team on both sides of the ball. Some fans joked it was beginning to feel as though the tougher competition had been found in the Colonial League.

Selinsgrove starters finally got on the scoreboard against the Panther reserves with three minutes and fifteen seconds remaining in the game. But the Saucon backups showed feisty resolve in not making it easy for the Seals. The final score of this game was Saucon Valley 35–Selinsgrove 7.

Thatcher averaged ten yards per carry, running ten times for 103 yards. He was also four of seven for fifty yards passing, including the touchdown to Harka. Defensively, the Panthers continued to impress. Selinsgrove had the reputation of putting up scary numbers against their opponents all season, however, their offense left with a whimper against this determined Panther "D." Saucon limited the explosive Juvon Batts to seventy-one yards on thirteen carries and Logan Leiby managed only seven of nineteen passes for one hundred yards. Thirty of those passing yards came on his touchdown throw against the JV team in the waning moments of the game.

Evan Culver spent the first twelve weeks of the season chewing up District 11 opponents and thanking his teammates every step of the way. He did the same in Saucon Valley's PIAA Class AAA regional playoff games, giving credit to everyone around him. But there was a little something extra in his performance on this quarterfinal night and it showed. "When I scored a TD, I just had to forget it and move on to the next play," said Culver, who finished with a school record 343 yards on just eighteen carries.

"The holes were there again, but Evan ran possessed tonight," Head Coach Matt Evancho said. "He worked for a lot more. He pushed past it. He ran like a man tonight."

The Panther defense had limited the Seals record-setting running back, Juvon Batts, to forty-nine yards and held the District IV Champs scoreless until the second-team defense gave up a score to the Selinsgrove first team with three minutes and fifteen seconds left in the game.

"I think our defense played really well," said Kane. "That pick-six on the first play helped out with our confidence and we just carried that through the rest of the game."

Harka's touchdown catch tied him with Kane for the program's career-best sixteen. They were also tied for second place in career catches with sixty-eight. Wolfe had nearly returned an interception for a touchdown early in the fourth quarter but had stepped out of bounds after making the pick. Holub also had an interception, and Adam Hough recovered a kickoff fumble.

Selinsgrove did manage a blocked punt in the first quarter by Ethan Trautman, who also ran eleven yards for a first down on a fake punt in the third quarter. But the Seals could not sustain anything against this Panther defense. After the blocked punt, Selinsgrove drove to the Saucon Valley 8 yard line thanks in part to personal fouls against our boys. But the Panthers stuffed Batts on three consecutive running plays, then pressured Leiby into an incompletion on fourth down. "We really stepped up on that side of the ball," Culver said.

In his postgame speech, Coach Evancho told his players to enjoy the win with their family and friends. He also told them to be ready for Monday. The new week would bring preparation for the next challenge. The most meaningful game of the year would be against a big city school. Imhotep Charter came from Philadelphia and recruited their players from across the city. But beware Imhotep, the Panthers were on a roll and were headed your way. The only thing certain about this contest was that the Panthers would win and the Panthers would lose, for the mascot was the same for both teams.

The Saucon Valley faithful brought a whole lot of energy and enthusiasm Friday night in the PIAA quarterfinals. We had filled our section of the stands and were the noticeably louder crowd.

At his postgame huddle with the team on Friday night, Coach Evancho announced they would get Saturday off to enjoy and savor the big win against Selinsgrove while the staff began to break down video of Imhotep Charter.

Evancho Interview, Photo credit: Keith Riefenstahl, *Saucon Source*

The boys were indeed focused, loose, and looking forward to the next challenge.

They'd earned a rest.

We'd be returning to Bethlehem Area School District Stadium (Liberty). Technically, this wouldn't be a home game for Saucon Valley, even though the stadium stands just twelve miles from Hellertown city limits. So, the Panthers would play on in this postseason, never once playing on their home field.

The parents helped get everything going. Matt Evancho never asked, never needed to know. The parents were the ones who put together every send-off when the team went on the road to the playoffs, and they were the ones who brought the team back into town. Matt said, "That, to me, that was like the storybook right there. That brought closure on our own Friday Night Lights. That included every cliche of a small town. The bus rides. You know, it was fantastic to have all that support."

Coach Evancho was especially fond of Dwight Thompson, saying, "He was our custodian up at the locker room at home. He stands out in the game crowd, cheering us on. I made sure he got a medal. Every championship we won because he was part of our team. He was always supportive of the players and coaches. Dwight made it a point to get to the know the players and interact with them whenever he was around. Coach Sams made up a story about Dwight, where he played for Tamaqua High School, and he made every tackle one game for them. He shared that with the kids, and we asked Dwight to go along with it. The players were in awe. Great fun! Dwight is an amazing person and we were lucky to have him as a part of the program."

CHAPTER 21

WHO'S TEP?

They're big, they're fast, they're talented.
—Matt Evancho, Saucon Valley head coach

ED CHROMCZAK SAID, "We more or less stayed with the same game plan through the entire year. I'm an old school guy. You know, we're in the I-formation most of the year. I remember, around week eight, Matt coming up to me and saying, 'Hey, let's put in a couple more plays.' I said, 'Matt, we have fifty plays in the playbook now and only run twelve of them.' I said that's all we've been doing all year. We don't want to put in more. 'I guess you're right,' he said. 'Let's just keep doing what we're doing.' We averaged forty-seven points a game that year in the first ten games. So that's not too shabby."

It's good, good stuff. As a team captain, and a team leader, Carvis said, "The team really started to gel in camp. There's something to be said about the bonds you make by just being together so much, that sometimes you get so sick of each other. But at the same time you know that building relationships and making memories like that really can't be replaced. That's the beauty of small-town American football. We knew each other from the time we were in flags to 85 pounds, all the way up through middle school and high school. It was the same core group, give or take a few years there, but we knew what to expect from each other."

On Sunday, as the coaches put together their game plan, the players watched some video of Imhotep to get a feel for what they would be up against. Monday after school they had a light workout and walk through on the field. The coaches introduced the Imhotep formations and tendencies that they would likely see Friday night. For example, 37 percent of the time Imhotep would run "Counter" on first down from an "Ace-look."

As in the prior fourteen weeks, the boys focused on their opponent's data and skills. Following the offensive-defensive "show," the varsity team members were supposed to get a workout in the weight room. But, thanks to Ryan Meyers, the team was excused by Coach Evancho from the lift session. Meyers had won a bet Coach made with the varsity squad. If one of six preselected players could throw and hit the crossbar of the goalpost with a football from twenty-five yards away, then the team would be excused. Ya gotta mix in some fun with your hard work!

Bob Frey sat with me to reflect on this season. My question was, "How did you build support from the school, the parents and the community?" He answered simply, "Internal support came with the kids and their families. Kids were energetic. So it was organic. That extends out to their friends and more, family. Success on the field generates this progressively. What the team's all about started with that bond they had. Momentum built up to the Notre Dame game. With so many people at that game, the energy kept building. A large travel crowd went on the road to each away game. We filled the bleachers at Bethlehem Area School District (BASD) Stadium. Imhotep had less than a hundred fans in those seats."

Continuing, Bob said, "The team and townspeople were generally positive; the team mood was good. We felt we had a positive plan going into the Imhotep game. The players and coaches believed in themselves and each other. The mindset was that we were going to win. We prepared for it with that in mind. We scored right away and held our own at the beginning of the game."

Josh Popichak, publisher of the *Saucon Source* wrote:

> It's been a little while since I followed high school football closely. More accurately, it's been a little over 20 years, which is how long it's been since I was in the band and a student at Liberty High School, and (attended) practically every varsity football game for four years. Tonight I'm headed to see the Saucon Valley Panthers take on Imhotep Charter in the biggest football game in the district's history. I'm feeling a full-circle kind of feeling, and it feels good because of the camaraderie that comes from being a high school sports fan. I've realized that's something that's been missing from my life. Being a local journalist requires me to always keep a close eye on high school sports—but that's not the same thing as being emotionally invested in them.
>
> The 2015 Saucon Valley football team is something special—not just because of their incredible talent, and the way they've brought an entire community together, but also for convincing me it was OK to deposit my emotion in something bigger than myself. I didn't think I'd ever do that again. But I have, and it feels great.
>
> I'm not the only one who can say this. When I look around the packed stands at any football game I see people of all ages—including many older than me—with sparkles in their eyes. They are young again watching these gifted athletes play football with 110 percent of their hearts, united toward a common goal. It is something magical to see and something you won't experience watching the game on TV. It's Christmastime, and the season when we are reminded (frequently) to *believe*. I have found a new

reason to believe, thanks to our boys. I hope you have too. And I hope that regardless of what happens tonight, we all remember this feeling for a long time. Life is too short not to believe in something bigger than yourself.

Josh is a journalist and publisher who is committed to providing an open platform for objective online local news. Originally from Bethlehem, Pennsylvania, he has covered news in the Saucon Valley area of eastern Pennsylvania since 2005. In addition to publishing news on SauconSource.com, which he launched in 2014, he uses Facebook, Instagram, and other social media platforms to help inform an ever-growing number of reader-followers.

Gail Nolf looked back kindly on 2015 as a memorable year. "It's all interesting because people still say, 'Remember 2015.' It's like this time stamp on the town where if you say 2015 in reference to sports or football, people know you're talking about this team. The community came out, and people still talk about how the Saucon Valley stands were filled with emotion! In most games, we would look across the field and feel a sense of honor that we filled the stands on our side, from our little town. You'd look across the field at those other programs and see their fan base couldn't touch ours."

This Saucon Valley varsity football team had accomplished many "firsts" in their journey up to this moment, none more significant than their first trip to the PIAA State Semifinal Playoff Game. That in and of itself affords an opportunity for the winning team to advance and play in the PIAA State Championship Game in Hershey. Matt Evancho and Chris Labatch had been here before. Their team was here for the first time.

The Panthers worked hard in the preceding week to prepare for the biggest game of their lives. As they had done throughout the playoff season, Hellertown and Saucon Valley residents, families, teachers, fellow-students, friends and others involved in various businesses along Main Street geared up to give the local boys a hearty send-off as they departed the high school grounds for the Bethlehem Area School District Stadium. Some have included videos on their websites in the years since of these parades as the team buses departed Hellertown and when they returned after those victories. You may also find some of the game film online, showing highlight reels of these guys playing the game they loved. It's worth it to watch again!

The players and coaches prepared this week just like it was any other week. Spotting a championship on the horizon and working through a routine proven to deliver success, the boys from Saucon Valley were once again ready to take on the beast!

Game Day

On this afternoon, Friday, December 11, 2015, team buses departed the school district campus around 4:30 p.m., riding north on Route 412 along Main Street to the Liberty High School Football Stadium in Bethlehem. Residents, workers, and customers along the route came out to wish them well with cheers and noise as their police-escorted convoy passed by.

The mild weather forecast held up, with a high in the upper fifties for game time.

A very large crowd of hometown supporters filled the west side of the stadium and, just as in the prior two BECA games at this same stadium, Saucon Valley fans sat together while the opposing team's fans left large gaps of space between them, like they didn't want to get too close to each other. A testimony to the close-knit community of the homegrown team contrasted with the "recruitment" atmosphere of the city team from Philadelphia.

For those not able to make it in person, viewing options were provided by local TV stations. RCN broadcast the game live on Channel 4 and Service Electric aired it live on its Channel 50 (Channel 550 in high definition).

In recent weeks football fever had taken a strong hold over

Hellertown, where groups sold red and black bows to decorate homes and businesses, raising funds for youth sports. Bows were sold at Pondelek's Florist & Gifts on Main St. (profits sent to the Saucon Valley Athletic Association and the Hellertown Historical Society). From Andy's and Pennewell's Florist on Main St., the first bow was free, and donations were accepted for additional bow purchases. Saucon Valley Football Boosters sold bows.

A colorful spirit and lots of emotion, hopes, and dreams from the hometown!

A local deli, the Hellertown Lunch Box, created two sandwiches to celebrate the occasion: the *Panther* named for the team and the *Heavenly Hog* named for the Hogs.

Imhotep Charter, known as "TEP," is an inner-city Philadelphia team who was also undefeated at 13–0. Aside from playing football, dominating their respective seasons, and a common Panther mascot, some might say the similarities between the two teams end there.

Wild panthers generally aren't social animals and don't live in family units. They are strong, quick, solitary creatures that hunt and eat. These very large Panthers coming in from the city were also strong, quick, and the hunting type.

According to their school website, "Imhotep Institute Charter High School is an African Centered science, mathematics, and technology learning community whose mission is to provide a standards driven, high quality educational program for urban learners grounded in the African Principles of MA'AT, a set of ethical and moral principles that originated in ancient Egypt. The seven principles of the Nguzo Saba serve as guidelines for building a strong and unified African American community. Imhotep aims to nurture lifelong learners who are valuable members of the world community. Principles surround family, community awareness, and togetherness."

There's another similarity between the two Panther squads; family, community awareness, and togetherness.

TEP—an undeniably physically imposing team—was now the

only obstacle blocking Saucon Valley's dream of a first-ever state football championship game.

Friday's highly anticipated PIAA semifinal showdown would determine whose dream came true with a trip to Hershey in the week before Christmas: TEP or Saucon.

In any event, Panthers would win and Panthers would lose.

Imhotep Charter had advanced to this round by soundly beating Academy Park 46–16 at Plymouth-Whitemarsh on December 4.

According to CBS Philly, TEP was hoping to become the first Philadelphia Public League team to win a PIAA state football championship.

MaxPreps had Imhotep Charter ranked at number five in the state football rankings of all teams, while Saucon Valley was ranked number seven overall (Parkland, playing at the AAAA level was ranked number one). The website ranked TEP number one and Saucon Valley number two among AAA teams.

TEP quarterback Nasir Boykin averaged 177.3 passing yards per game versus Saucon quarterback Zach Thatcher's 79.3 yards.

TEP averaged 198.3 rushing yards per game compared to Saucon's 385.5 yards per game.

TEP had six players who weighed more than three hundred pounds on its current roster, with the biggest tipping the scales at 368 pounds. Saucon Valley's largest player was three-hundred-pound junior Tackle Cody Zrinski. Leading their way to the TEP buffet was senior guard Johncarlo Valentin at six feet, five inches, 338 pounds. His classmate Yasir Durant was listed at six feet, seven inches, 328 pounds. Sophomore Justin Johnson checked in at six feet, seven inches, 324 pounds. Senior Jahmir Johnson measured six feet, five inches, 272 pounds, while the runt of the litter was junior center Brashon McRae at six feet, two inches, and only 257 pounds. It would be safe to say this group was among the biggest offensive line units in the nation. Matt Evancho remembered watching Thursday night NFL football on TV the night before this game, and the Texans were playing. They put their starting offensive line on the screen, and he noted that Imhotep had a bigger offensive line than the Texans. That was the reality of this game. One of TEP's players went on to play at Penn State, another went to Florida State. Their best running back didn't play due to an injury suffered the week before. His backup already had a Division I offer to play for Arizona.

In addition to their size, TEP also had speed. The Saucon Valley coaches expected to see Mike Waters hauling the pigskin out of the backfield for Imhotep. He was listed at five feet, ten inches tall, and 190 pounds. As a backup to injured Tyliek Raynor, who had broken his ankle in their playoff win the prior week, Waters had rushed for over one thousand yards. Junior Nasir Boykin was a dual threat quarterback with speed as well. Boykin was listed at six feet, one inch, and 184 pounds.

Imhotep Game, Photo credit: Keith Riefenstahl, *Saucon Source*

TEP Charter had some high-profile Division I recruits led by Shaka Toney (Penn State) and Naseir Upshur (Florida State). Saucon Valley had just one, tight end Mike Kane.

Matt Evancho's team would have to be really good again Friday night, bringing their A game. They could not afford to make mistakes.

"They're big, they're fast, they're talented," Evancho said of the District XII champions. "But I like how we're playing. I feel confident in what our guys can do."

What Saucon Valley had done successfully before was jump on teams early, outscoring opponents 394–92 in the first half of all their wins that season.

TEP had done similar work, making it interesting to see how Friday night's trailing team would respond. Neither team had trailed their opponents this season, although Saucon Valley had to break a tie in order to win game eight.

"It's extremely important to [score first]," senior Receiver Nate Harka said. "They haven't been punched in the face. To score first would shoot them back to reality."

The District XI Champions needed to maintain their composure, limit emotional penalties, and play a complete game. "Teams have been trying to get us to retaliate and some of us do," Zrinski said. "That puts us in a third-and-fifteen [situation], and that hurts us."

Evancho was pleased with how focused his team had been the previous Friday against Selinsgrove, particularly in the second half. Saucon Valley had two personal fouls in the first half, but efficiently put away Selinsgrove in the third quarter.

TEP had not given in to such temptation with late hits, verbal sparring with officials, or opposing teams. "[Imhotep] is very disciplined," Evancho said. "They play the game the right way. They don't get personal fouls, stupid penalties. You're going to see two different styles but similar philosophies in coaching, how to play the game the right way."

When TEP was at its best, it generated big plays offensively behind its massive offensive line, creating room for a talented set of backs led by senior running back Mike Waters.

Waters averaged 11.4 yards per carry and had the Philadelphia

Public League single-season record with thirty-seven touchdowns. Quarterback Nasir Boykin was averaging 21.9 yards per completion.

"They mix it up well," Evancho said of coach Albie Crosby's Panthers. "They throw the ball early, on third down, in short yardage, long yardage. They like to throw screen passes. Their receivers are good. They are able to get yards after the catch. We'll have to get to the ball, make the tackle."

Saucon Valley needed to win the battle at the line of scrimmage to prevent Waters and others from busting off big plays. Saucon's defensive front line would try to create havoc in the TEP backfield. Linebackers Christian Carvis and others knew they couldn't overpursue against their speedy runners who are capable of breaking tackles and reversing field.

"We have to get to the point of attack before they get to us," Evancho said. "If we play smart, we can make some things happen. If we don't and let them get to us first, we're going to be in trouble."

Saucon Valley had made a season of its own big plays on offense and putting together lengthy, time-consuming drives wouldn't be the worst alternative.

But Saucon Valley would need to finish those drives.

Evancho's bunch also needed to find ways to get its defense off the field as fast as possible to avoid being worn down by TEP's decided size advantage.

"We need to execute, not make mistakes, stop them on third down, and minimize their big plays," Harka said. "We've got to stop the run and go from there."

Saucon Valley had gone from a competitive Colonial League to District XI playoff command, to state regional tournament domination, to state semifinalist in two years because the players had committed themselves to the program and one another. Saucon Valley had conquered many talented teams that season with their cohesiveness and discipline as much as their talent.

Zrinski was asked a few times in 2015 by people outside of the

Saucon program if the Panthers could win this game. He had been surprised each time by the suggestion of the question. "Do you think?" he said. "I know [we can win]."

The winner would advance to the state finals in Hershey against the Bishop McDevitt-Erie Cathedral Prep winner. A loss would bring the dream to an end.

TEP ran a base 4-4 defense that would often look like a 4-3 based on Saucon's formations. The entire defense played very fast and closed holes quickly. They liked pressuring up the middle with Upshur and "spilling" the run to their speed outside.

TEP had only given up sixty-eight points in thirteen games, with eight shutouts. This was notably the biggest, fastest, and most dominating unit Saucon had faced all year. The Hogs, Thatcher, Culver, Kane, Carvis, and their teammates would have their hands full.

TEP showed multiple looks from a standard "twins" set to a variety of spread looks. They first tried to establish the run behind their mammoth offensive line that liked to run "power" and "counter." When they ran power, it was typically with 338 pounds pulling and leading through the hole. When it is "counter" we would see about 650 pounds leading the way. TEP also had the speed outside to stretch the field and run a variety of quick "bubble" and "rocket" screen passes. They had hurt their opponents by splitting their tight end Upshur out wide and letting Boykin throw the deep fade. TEP liked to pound the ball but could also make plays with their passing game horizontally and vertically. It was a versatile, well-balanced attack.

Saucon Valley entered the game as the heavy underdog. It would be the biggest challenge of the season for Saucon to overcome. It might get bloody. It would definitely be a grind.

When we saw the two teams take the field, the first thought that came to mind was *boys against men*. Imhotep Charter, would not easily be conquered, yet we found consolation in the old adage,

"The harder the conflict, the more glorious the triumph."

Not many people outside of the Saucon Valley area were giving our boys much of a chance against that heavyweight team. On paper, Imhotep Charter's appearance of a high school football program was just too well-constructed to overcome. The task was too tall against this stacked deck. But what Imhotep may not have had, that turned out to be the difference-maker for Saucon Valley, was an authentic sense of homegrown brotherhood and family. A sense of community ran deep through the core of our players, an inner-belief and confidence that could subconsciously carry the day.

Both Teams Are In It To Win It
On the game's first play, TEP's Amir Brown took the opening kickoff and weaved his way eighty-four yards through Saucon Valley special teams players for the opening touchdown. First time for everything! Their two-point conversion succeeded, posting a score of 8–0 within the first few seconds of the game. Boom! What had just happened? This was going to be a race.

Saucon Valley hunkered down and got accustomed to their speedy opponent.

Thatcher took our kickoff back. Catching the game's second kickoff in under thirty seconds, he ran up the middle and got tackled in a pile. One of the TEP tacklers grabbed Thatcher's groin, letting it be known that this was going to be a game played by "city rules."

Senior fullback Mike Paolini took a handoff on the first play from scrimmage, racing fifty-two yards for a first down. That set up Culver's three-yard touchdown run on the following play, and with Snead's extra point, pulled the locals within one at 8–7 one minute into the game. That surprised TEP, as no one had scored so easily on them.

Ending the first quarter, down ten 24–14, this was as close as Saucon Valley would get. The thirty-eight points scored in the first quarter were the most rung up in a state semifinal game up to that point in time in PIAA history. Bittersweet, but another first.

Later, Thatcher's forty-eight-yard touchdown run got Saucon Valley to within two scores at five minutes and twenty-six seconds left in the second quarter, 32–20. But the visiting Panthers scored the game's next six touchdowns, leaving no doubt about who would go on to play in Hershey.

Saucon Valley was hurt by four lost fumbles, more than its previous fourteen-game total, and one interception. TEP took advantage of those five turnovers, scoring eighteen points. TEP scored nine offensive touchdowns on thirty-six plays and had two other touchdowns—one on special teams that was called back because of penalties.

Saucon Valley couldn't keep up with their opponent's version of speed and elusiveness. "They were very fast," Saucon Valley coach Matt Evancho said. "We knew that. But to be able to do what they did, start and stop on a dime then reverse. It was a special skill we had not been up against. When we thought we had them, they were gone."

TEP's Mike Waters scored on touchdown runs of three, seventy-six, forty-seven, and four yards—all in a five-carry stretch. He also hauled in a forty-eight-yard scoring pass to give TEP a 60–20 lead at the break.

Saucon Valley had gotten their lunch handed to them, and the second half was played under the mercy rule.

Culver ran for seventy-three yards and two touchdowns to finish his record-setting season with 2,934 yards and forty-eight scores, both school records. At graduation, his total season yardage ranked fifth best in District XI history. His TD total tied for third highest in the district annals. Culver ended his career with 4,937 yards, eleventh all-time in District XI.

Through it all, Saucon Valley received tremendous support from their fans, who parked in the west stands, watching this game from the opening kickoff to the last whistle. The sustained applause given to the team as they walked off the field has remained with the players all these years.

It was a sign of just how far the Saucon Valley program had come the last three years. "The crowd was awesome," Evancho said. "No matter what. Things didn't go the way we wanted, but they loved us through the end. What we've created was huge."

The greatest run in Saucon Valley school football history had ended. Bu what a ride.

And oh, what memories!

Even though the result didn't turn out the way it was planned, we made friendships, won awards, rode spontaneous parades. The whole town supported us, and these memories say it was all worth the journey. This sentiment was echoed by coaches, players and parents.

Their best efforts and the enthusiastic support of an entire community were not enough to overcome the athletic prowess of their Philadelphia opponent, Imhotep Charter. The team lost 72–27, after posting the highest point total against TEP that season.

It took an oversized, electric team from the second largest city in the state to knock us off. All of Saucon's points were posted in the first half against their starters, but we were still shut down in the second. Little consolation and small a footnote in history.

Some observers said the matchup was unfair, since TEP was able to recruit its players from a wide metropolitan area while Saucon's football talent was entirely homegrown.

This team went further than any other squad in Saucon Valley School District's history, and along the way captured the hearts of their community.

On the way to and from Bethlehem Area School District Stadium they were escorted by local police, fire, and EMS personnel in their colorful vehicles with horns blaring. Our boys were welcomed back home as heroes.

Hundreds of residents turned out along the route from the high school to the Freemansburg Steel City bridge to cheer for the team on their return trip to the school. And many more were at the high school when the Panther escort arrived a little after 10 p.m.

On Facebook, hundreds of supportive comments were posted by fans who told the team how proud they were of what they had accomplished that year.

"Congratulations Saucon players!" wrote Chris Guro. "David couldn't beat Goliath this time, but you gave the most valiant effort possible! Thanks for making the sacrifices and commitment to make it to this level of play!"

"Great job Saucon! Couldn't be prouder!" added Kelly Opitz Buki.

Alicia Kichline commented, "So proud of them! That was a very tough team with boys on there that were bigger than NFL players." Kichline wrote, "We still fought and tried our best and that is the most important part!"

Keith Riefenstahl even commented. "Great job guys! Your efforts gave the Saucon Valley community a season of memories that will last forever. You revitalized and energized this sleepy little town. We are forever proud of what you accomplished and how you went about it. Your 2015 season will be legendary! The Community is with you!"

Thatcher reflected, saying, "We hung with them for a while. It was basically like 27–20 until they opened up. We caught lightning in a bottle and then once that opening kickoff was over, it kind of left. But it was a really fun game." Zach was named Player of the Game at the Saucon Valley banquet, later in the year. That really meant a lot to him because that was a really interesting game that was never going to happen again. He remembered looking at the fans in the seats. "It seemed that literally all of Hellertown was there."

The following article for LehighValleyLive.com was written by Greg Joyce.

> The game had been over for a few minutes by the clock, longer by what the scoreboard said, but the Saucon Valley football team stood once more to a roar from its faithful crowd.
>
> Someone could have robbed a bank in Hellertown

Friday night and nobody would have known, because the entire borough was seemingly in the home stands at Bethlehem Area School District Stadium.

And even as Imhotep Charter scored again and again on the way to a 72–27 win, the crowd never thinned, as if it was saying thank you to the Panthers for bringing them along on this ride to the PIAA Class AAA semifinals.

The 2015 Saucon Valley football team went where no other had gone before in program history, finishing the season 14–1 as Colonial League champs, District 11 champs and one game away from the state championship.

"It's just amazing," senior offensive lineman/linebacker Christian Carvis said. "(The crowd) stuck with us, even when we were down 40 points, it didn't matter. They were with us the whole time. That speaks volumes about our community and that speaks about the character of our program and what kind of stuff we've built in the last couple years."

When Carvis and his classmates were freshmen, the Panthers went 4–7. Then they helped put together 9–3 and 10–2 seasons, but none compared to this one.

This Saucon Valley team evoked signs of support and encouragement up and down Main Street in Hellertown. The further the Panthers went into uncharted territory in the postseason, the more signs that went up.

Before the game, a multitude of encouraging tweets were sent out to Saucon Valley from fellow Colonial League or District 11 teams, even teams from outside the area, all rooting for the small-town school to pull off the big-time upset.

It didn't happen, but their fans still came out in droves for their hope to keep the dream alive.

"What else can you say about that? That's awesome,"

coach Matt Evancho said. "It didn't go the way we wanted but they loved us till the end. What we've created there I think is going to be huge from here on out. We just have to build off of that."

Doing that is going to be a tough task, but the idea of going to the state semifinals or beyond, which may have once sounded like a dream, became a reality in 15 Fridays or Saturdays this fall. The foundation has now been laid by this year's group of 14 seniors.

"They're amazing," an emotional Evancho said. "This group, I love them. It's going to be tough to replace this group. But I know what they've done for the program and for the town is amazing. I don't think any other town has had this happen to them, like what we've done.

"This junior group and the sophomores, they have big shoes to fill. A lot of them are ready to do that, and I know they're probably ready tomorrow, but we gotta take some time off."

Senior running back Evan Culver leaves as the program's leading rusher, both in season (2,934) and career (4,937) yards. He also finished the year with a program-record 48 touchdowns (and 77 for his career), moving into a tie for third-place all time in the District 11 single-season record books.

Senior quarterback Zach Thatcher left with more than 1,000 yards rushing and 1,000 yards passing, second in career passing touchdowns (31).

Senior wide receiver Nate Harka broke the program's career receiving yards record with 1,302, along with the career receiving touchdowns record with 17. His 30-yard score Friday night broke the tie with senior tight end Mike Kane, who is the school's all-time sack leader.

Carvis leaves as the program's season and career

tackling record-breaker, while being a part of the offensive line that cleared the way for more than 5,000 rushing yards.

Fullback/linebacker Mike Paolini and wide receiver/defensive back Adam Hough also played critical roles to help this team reach the big stage.

All of the senior offensive starters were pulled from the game with two minutes to go so that the crowd could recognize them once more with a standing ovation from the bleachers and big hugs from coaches on the sideline.

The Panthers had rewarded them with the season of a lifetime, one that they'll be talking about in Hellertown for a long time to come. And even amidst the tears Friday night, they were already able to appreciate what they had done.

"I couldn't ask for a better senior year, I couldn't ask for a better group of kids to be around, I couldn't ask for a better coaching staff," Carvis said. "I love everyone in the program. I love the community, the students, the whole school. They've been behind us the whole way. Can't ask for anything better, 14–1."

Saucon Valley's Matt Evancho is the 2015 Lehigh Valley Live Football Coach of the Year."

Recap

Saucon Valley went into that game with a belief that we could win. There was no doubt, when you looked those players in the eye, they felt we could win. We knew it wasn't going to be easy. Giving up the opening kickoff for a touchdown did not start well, but that wasn't the gameplan. We came right back. On our second play from scrimmage, Paolini ran the option play down to the 1 yard line. So we were right there, we were right back in it. It was tough. Even though the situation we were in posed a little bit of uncertainty, there was never any quit in this team.

This game gave them an opportunity to really see firsthand what they had accomplished. The starters and especially the seniors were able to get an ovation coming off the field. And it was a moment they deserved because they put in a lot of time, effort, and sweat to get to get to that point.

Trained well.

Worked hard.

Accomplished much.

Matt Evancho said solemnly, "I don't want to forget that game, honestly. Because I think we showed a lot of character. Looking back, I'd like to do some things a little differently throughout the year, but for the most part, I wouldn't change anything. I think it took a while to accept this. I've been ducking this conversation for a while. Things happened after that season in my personal life. I try not to go back a lot. But I've come to a point now where the strength is there to do a little more, face those things head on, allow myself to move past it. But I would not change anything about that football season. Following some of my own advice, it's time to move on."

This Saucon Source photo says so much! Here Head Coach Matt Evancho hugs his daughter, watching the players in a team huddle following Imhotep loss.

CHAPTER 22

BEYOND 2015

There's no question the relationships with my student athletes were the most rewarding. Being there through thick and thin, witnessing their development into young men—that's what truly matters.
—Matt Evancho, Saucon Valley head coach

THIS CHAMPIONSHIP RUN wouldn't have been possible without the unwavering dedication of every team member. From the coaches who held true to the operational strategy to the support staff ensuring every need was met to the players who left their hearts on the field, the team assembled by Bob Frey and Matt Evancho built this legacy. Together, they wrote a remarkable chapter in Saucon Valley's history, one that will be remembered for years to come.

The guys on the field, those you watched and cheered on, and read so much about during their playing days have accomplished much in addition to winning ball games. They've become men with good character. After all is said and done, that's why they do what they do.

Regular season record-setting performances from the Panthers included Evan Culver becoming the all-time leading rusher and scorer in school history. He passed former teammate Nick Savant, who had finished his career two years earlier as the previous top dog. Several other teammates set new standards. Josh Snead became the single-season record holder for extra points. Christian Carvis tied the team's single-season tackle assist total. Mike Kane became the career sack leader.

More Than a Coach, a Mentor

Staying connected with his coaching family was a priority for Matt Evancho. He cherishes these relationships built in the trenches together. They understand the unique challenges coaches face—the exhilarating victories and the crushing defeats. Coach Evancho still makes a point to catch up with them regularly, offering support and sharing the camaraderie that only those who've been in the game can understand.

A smile spread across his face while talking about Chris Labatch, "We were close back then and now it's a bond that transcends coach and player. We talk almost every day, with him seeking advice, me seeing him as a son. It's a privilege to watch this dynamic unfold with others as well. There's no question about it," his voice filling with pride.

Ed Chromczak stood out as a constant presence during Evancho's tenure at Saucon Valley. "It was just Ed and me through my whole tenure at that school," Evancho reflects. "Others came and went, some returning later. But Ed, he's a rock. I can't express how much that man means to me personally. He was like a father figure, a trusted advisor, and a mentor—not just for me, but for the younger coaches too. In 2015, we had a lot of fresh faces on the staff and if you think about it, we were coaching coaches as well as the players." Two—Labatch and Phil Sams—went on to become head coaches at other Colonial League schools. Chromczak, also at another Colonial League school, continues to coach the line—a calling he has been committed to for more than thirty years.

College-Bound

"I believe that year was a turning point," Karen Kane said, reflecting on 2015. "It seems like it was the first year the *Morning Call* sports editor really took notice of our football team." Perhaps our boys surprised a lot of people, but their character and talent couldn't be ignored.

Their success translated into opportunities for several players.

"At least eight of them went on to play college football," Karen said, beaming with pride as she rattled off names: "Mike, Nate, Evan, Zach, Christian, Cody, Ryan, and Alstan."

A hint of wistfulness crept into Evancho's voice. "It felt surreal when they first graduated college. Hearing about their careers, it suddenly dawned on me—they're all grown up now. Part of me still sees them in their jerseys, fired up and ready to play. That final game, that's my lasting memory—their transformation not just as athletes, but as individuals."

He continued, growing more nostalgic. "I think one thing that was always something I really liked and enjoyed was having my kids there to be a part of it. That was special. In one game, my daughter somehow got herself on the field. She's yelling at the officials, and I turned to yell at her to get back. It didn't even dawn on me, like, why is she down here? But just having them as a part of it made it even better."

The players Matt expressed admiration for all spoke highly of his leadership and coaching style, how he nurtured their development. Those lessons learned have stayed with them. They're all becoming fine young men. Their legacy starts in the next chapter.

Lessons Beyond the Game

Reminiscing about his college days, Matt revealed, "My coach constantly emphasized a crucial message—football teaches you skills that go beyond those four years. It's a philosophy I'm grateful my son experiences at his school too. They focus on building a foundation for life."

He leaned forward, his voice taking on a deeper tone. "And those life lessons translate into adulthood. The camaraderie forged on the field—your teammates, coaches, friends, and family—becomes a support system you can always rely on, even when things get tough."

He paused thoughtfully. "For me," he continued, "the key was staying focused on the process, on building something bigger than ourselves. I also made a conscious effort to empower my assistant coaches, allowing them to connect with the players in their own unique way. It fostered a sense of family within the team."

A chuckle escaped his lips. "Take Coach Chromczak, for example. He had this gruff exterior, but the players knew his heart was gold. It was always amusing to see Cody Zrinski and Ryan Meyers try to get under his skin, pushing his buttons almost daily."

Resignation

Evancho called his assistant coaches one Monday night to share the news with them, then called a meeting for his team just after homeroom on Tuesday morning at school. He had always asked his players to be honest with him. He wanted to be the same with them, and to do that, he had to tell them what he had been going through over the last twenty-plus years.

The truth was that football needed to take a backseat to real life, to his two kids and wife at home. And the truth was that Evancho had been battling depression since his college days at Penn State, maybe even before that. He didn't really know yet. That was the side he had yet to uncover.

But this was Evancho on a Tuesday morning in December 2015, telling his players that he was hanging up the whistle. After leading the Panthers to the PIAA Class AAA semifinals, he stepped down because, after putting so much time into football, it was time to stop avoiding what he had known deep down for some time.

"It kind of just hit me in the face that it's time to take care of this," Evancho said. "I didn't want anything to be hidden. This is what I am. This is who I am. I have to face that now and work through that."

For leading Saucon Valley to unprecedented heights with Colonial League and District XI titles, capped by a trip to the state semifinals, Evancho became the 2015 Lehigh Valley Live Football Coach of the Year. But for his players, he was much more.

There's the notion that football players and coaches must be tough, and also the negative stigma around mental illnesses and that having one shows weakness. But Evancho, a football lifer, showed overriding courage when he opened up to his team.

"Mental illness is no different than any other illness you're battling," Evancho said. "It's just that nobody wants to look at it. They think just because you admit that, you're weak."

About 6.7 percent of American adults live with depression, according to the National Alliance on Mental Illness. In 2013, an estimated 2.6 million kids ages twelve to seventeen had at least one major depressive episode—about one in ten kids in the United States—according to the National Institute of Mental Health.

Yet far less actually seek help or get the proper treatment. Evancho had been included in that category until that year. He gave it his all. He left his heart on the field working with teenagers on a daily basis, knowing how much it could affect them.

"I know there's a lot of kids with depression and I just want to make sure they understand it's not a negative," Evancho said. "There are plenty of people that deal with it and I'm no different than them. We have to find support in each other.

"For a group of people that know and trust in me, hopefully I can make something better for somebody, help out someone."

But in order to help any of the kids he coached or taught every day, he had to first help himself.

Before the Panthers' magical season even began, Evancho started to come to terms with what was going on. Over the summer, he had some of his worst moments. He realized it, talked to doctors and then had to think about the upcoming football season—the hours upon hours that would be spent on the field and in the locker room and all the responsibilities in between.

Evancho didn't want to "just get through" the season. He had to commit himself to his team. He needed to make sure he was going to be there for them because he wasn't just a coach to them; he had become like a second father to many, and in return, he had fifty sons. Many high school coaches experience similar struggles.

"It's not just technique; it's about being a husband, being a father that he's taught us," senior captain Christian Carvis said. "It's stuff like that that'll stick with me for the rest of my life."

They had asked their coach to help them be the best they could be and then they would give him everything they had. Evancho wanted to deliver that same promise.

"I wasn't going to turn my back on the kids," the Easton grad said.

After much soul-searching about what he had to do next, Matt Evancho eventually resigned on the heels of the team's most successful season ever. He was going out on top but nurturing a deep emotional pain!

"I wanted them to hear it straight from me. I've always been that way," he said about his career-changing decision. "I needed time for myself, time for my family, to look at where I was, what I was doing and to take care of myself for a change." And it was important that at that time with my kids getting older, I had to take that step. I loved coaching and working with the kids, but I felt it was time for me to take a break. With my daughter, Kayla, at Easton cheering on Friday nights, there was no way I could miss being there. I think the biggest highlights would be how much community support the team received this year. It was magical and just like you would see in a movie. The players and coaches will never forget that." Evancho continued as an assistant coach for his son's youth basketball team while getting to watch his daughter cheerleading. His first priority now became his family and the personal care that he needed.

Evancho left the door open for a return to coaching somewhere down the road. "I don't know when that will be," he said in 2015. "I just know it's probably not going to be very soon. It's probably going to be a little bit of time because I need Friday nights to myself for a while. I need to see where that goes."

And for the first time in a while, that was okay with Matt Evancho. It was no longer about what more he had to do. He enjoyed the ride with his football team this time around, and then he was off to commit to a deeper cause.

Athletic Director Bob Frey issued his official statement, "It is with heartfelt regret that the Saucon Valley School District and Saucon Valley Athletic Department accepts the resignation of Mr. Matt Evancho as our Head Football Coach."

Frey went on to say, "In his tenure at Saucon Valley, Coach Evancho has taught his players the importance of many life lessons; dedication, hard work and commitment. It is Coach Evancho's emphasis on building character, respect, sportsmanship and dedication to family that will be his lasting impact on the Saucon Valley Football program. Coach Evancho's choice to dedicate time to his family is the driving force in his decision and his choice to practice what he teaches our players and students. The last nine years, but especially the 2015 football season was one in which the Hellertown and Lower Saucon communities will not soon forget."

Coach Evancho continued on for several years as a member of the Saucon Valley family, teaching and assisting the boys Lacrosse coach.

As we've seen, Evancho led the Panthers on a memorable journey. In addition to being a record-setter as the winningest coach in Saucon Valley history, he directed the Panthers to a pair of Eastern Conference championships (2007 and 2013) and a pair of Colonial League championships (2014 and 2015). Additionally, the 2015 Panthers won the District XI title and advanced to the semifinals of the PIAA state championships.

Soon after, Coach Evancho earned a United States Marine Corps honor. The Marine Corps and a nationwide organizer of football clinics, Colorado Springs based Glazier Football Clinics, showed they, too, thought Evancho's work mattered.

They honored Evancho with the Semper Fi Award during a meeting of the Saucon Valley School Board. Evancho said, "It is definitely something I enjoyed sharing with the team. My success is due to their success, as well. It was a group effort and we all had a part in it."

It's not the winning (61–43) record that Evancho's varsity football teams compiled that caught the eye of the Marine Corps and Glazier Football Clinics, according to the presenters. It was the way his approach modeled the Marines' leadership values of honor, courage, and commitment. I can't help but think that his mentor at Wilson Area High, Marine Corps veteran Bret Comp, had something to do with Matt's development in this regard.

"He was one of forty-three coaches across the United States chosen in 2015 to receive the award through the program, then in its fifth year. Previous winners with ties to the Lehigh Valley region were Jason Strunk, a Northampton Area High School graduate and head football coach at Lubbock High School in Texas, in 2014 and Warren Hills Regional High School coach Larry Dubiel in 2013. The coaches recognized with the award exemplify the Marine Corps' motto of Semper Fi—always faithful," said Marine Corporal Matthew S. Myers.

Evancho was chosen from among coaches in the Corps' Recruiting Station Harrisburg territory that encompasses Lehigh, Northampton, Bucks, Philadelphia, Chester, Lancaster, Dauphin, Schuylkill, Carbon, Wyoming, Wayne, Pike, Monroe, and Berks counties, Myers said.

"I just feel it's a great honor people recognize the hard work that coaches put in," Evancho said. "Many of us, if not all of us, don't do it for the recognition. But to be recognized in a special way like this, it was a great honor."

Bob Frey, the school district's athletic director, described Evancho as an excellent role model, and a father-figure to his student-athletes.

"One of the things that came out of this season, just beyond the success on the field, is just how he carries himself on and off the field," Frey said. "It's just awesome to see someone like that get well-deserved recognition."

Evancho said that as he enjoyed more time with his family away from the football field, he continued to advocate for more discussion surrounding mental illness.

He hopes others who may be struggling see his situation and that it's possible to get help.

"I think we really need to do that and help people," he said.

Finding a New Passion in Broadcasting
Transitioning into sports broadcasting within a year of his retirement, Evancho began his new career alongside Al DeCarlo, calling Friday night and Saturday afternoon games for Service Electric. This sparked his interest in sports media. Al now runs his own live streaming platform, sponsored by St. Luke's. What sets these two broadcasts apart? Student journalists from participating high schools contribute to the platform. They write articles, interview coaches, and players, and gain valuable experience in sports journalism. Matt, always the teacher and coach, enjoys mentoring them.

Balancing Broadcasting with Officiating
In 2022, he began officiating football games primarily at the subvarsity level. This keeps him connected to the game on Fridays when he's not broadcasting and Saturdays when he's not attending his son's college games. Officiating also offers a unique perspective on the sport. He sees the game from a different perspective now, interacting with coaches as an official. There is more empathy for them, having been a coach himself. That helps him excel in officiating and consider a potential return to coaching someday.

Evancho admits he underestimated the complexity of officiating rules compared to coaching. He sees the value of officiating crews where teammates can rely on each other. However, not all officials have coaching experience, so, maybe there's another mentoring opportunity?

When asked about his favorite role—coaching, officiating, or broadcasting—Matt's answer depends on the day. He misses the camaraderie of coaching during the season (August to December) but not the off-season demands. Officiating and broadcasting fill some of the void left from coaching by providing a different kind of adrenaline rush and remaining connected to the sport he loves.

CHAPTER 23

LEGACY

You can win, win, win, but if you're not equipping young men to be great husbands and fathers, you lose.
—Dabo Swinney, Clemson Head Football Coach

FROM COVER TO cover in this historical account of the heritage established by this team; coaches, staff and players, we leave a lasting legacy of leadership principles which translated to success on and off the field.

Benefits of Teaching and Coaching
Teaching and coaching in the same place has its advantages. Coaches get to know the kids on a deeper level—their strengths, weaknesses, and personalities. This knowledge translates seamlessly from the classroom to the field, allowing a connection as both a teacher and a coach. Sams had a lot of fun as an assistant coach, and it's clear he values the relationships built with those players.

Sams said that when Coach Evancho tendered his notice,

> Chris and I talked about who wanted to put in for the open position. And I said, 'Listen, man. I want to be a head football coach someday. Does it have to be right now? No. It doesn't have to be.' And I think Chris really wanted the job. What ended up happening was that Chris took the open Wilson coaching job and kind of shocked some people. Then I put in for the Saucon Valley job and

you know, I was fortunate to get selected. It's not always fun to follow that kind of season, because the expectations are through the roof. Oh my gosh, how do we get back to finals? How do you follow a superstar? It's so much easier to take over program in the tank because expectations are so low. But the kids responded great. We followed 2015 by winning another Colonial League Championship and got right back to District XI finals. I got the head job at Southern Lehigh in 2020 and have been here ever since.

I haven't seen that same level of community excitement since. I can't remember the last time I saw people standing out, even for the first round of playoffs. During the 2015 season, Hellertown had a very tight community, and the people really cared. I was on the bus rides, saw the ribbons and fans supporting us, watched the fire trucks and police cruisers escorting us out all the way through Steel City. I can remember coming home late at night after a road trip and seeing people standing outside the bars, walking down Main Street waving with a beer in their hand. Like it was a really neat experience. My sons rode the bus, they were pretty young at the time. They would just stare out the window at this crazy atmosphere. And I honestly, personally, haven't seen that kind of community support before or since that year. You know, it's a great small-town, blue-collar town story.

The transition from high school to college football can be surprising for players. They're used to packed stadiums filled with cheering fans, a hallmark of high school Friday nights. College brings a different atmosphere, especially outside the top programs. Here, the love for the game itself becomes the driving force. The competition intensifies, but the electric atmosphere of high school spirit is often absent in Division II and Division III schools.

Coach Sams said, "That's a big reason why I've dedicated twenty-four years to coaching high school football. The energy in those small-town communities is unmatched. It's a unique camaraderie you just don't find elsewhere. There's a magic to Friday night lights, a sense of community cheering on their own. I experienced it myself when I first started coaching and it solidified my passion for this level of the game."

Sams emphasized that football success goes beyond the players and their families. It's about the entire community rallying behind the team. Schools like Southern Lehigh and Berwick historically excelled at maintaining this spirit. It's a challenge, but hopefully they can recapture that magic. Perhaps it's easier to sustain this intensity in smaller, tight-knit communities, where football might be a central focus.

Stand Up Guys
The 2015 Saucon Valley football team was known as a team that played with heart, but seven teammates showed what big hearts they have inside. These players arrived at Saucon

Photo credit: Keith Riefenstahl, Saucon Source

Valley Manor on Main Street to deliver several cartloads full of poinsettia plants to the residents, many of whom were shut in during the holidays and unable to partake in the simple joys of the Christmas season. Nate Harka, Cody Zrinski, Mike Kane, Christian Carvis, Steven Good, Trey Polak, and Ryan Meyers brought the poinsettias donated by Dan Schantz Greenhouse to the lobby of the assisted living facility in Hellertown for distribution by manor employees.

Normally the Saucon players delivered the poinsettias to the manor after their annual end-of-season banquet was held, but that year the banquet was put on hold while the team advanced deep into the PIAA state championship tournament.

Additionally, after their storybook season ended, the team captains penned the following heartfelt letter of appreciation and affection to their fans. What a class act!

> **We're So Proud to Call Saucon Valley Our Home**
>
> On behalf of our entire team, we would like to thank you for your incredible support throughout this past season. To our coaches, parents, teachers and administration, your guidance was irreplaceable. To our fans, the cheerleaders, band and "Jungle," thanks for cheering us on each and every week. To our local businesses, police and fire departments and EMS personnel, thanks for being behind us every step of the way.
>
> Without your support and encouragement, we would not have been able to achieve all that we did. Coming into this season we had great expectations for ourselves, and we were able to achieve our goals. With your support, we were able to go above and beyond what we could have ever imagined.
>
> As we got further into the season, more and more signs and decorations were put up throughout town.

It was a great way to show your support and we really appreciate it.

Finally, the sendoff that you gave us to the State Semi-final game was a surreal moment that we will remember forever. Being able to provide such excitement to this town helped us understand that we were playing for something bigger than ourselves. Although the game did not turn out as we had hoped, you cheered for us until the final whistle and provided us with an equally grand greeting when we returned to town. That is the part that is the most special because through good times or bad we knew you all would be there every step of the way. We cannot thank you enough for that. We're so proud to call Saucon Valley our home! Go Panthers!"

Zach Thatcher, Evan Culver, Mike Kane, Christian Carvis (2012–2015)

Where Are They Now?
The Saucon Valley football team probably did more to bring that community together than anything. People who thought maybe the Colonial League just wasn't good began to see it wasn't a cakewalk. After Nick Savant powered his way through the league in 2012 and 2013, then graduated, his backup reached opposing team's end zones with disarming frequency, blowing away multiple school rushing records. All of a sudden you saw they had a great running back and a great quarterback. But how did they get there? The unsung heroes, guys up front were the teammates that really got things done, paving the way, making their blocks . . . Trey Polak, Cody Zrinski, Ryan Meyers, Christian Carvis, and Mike Kane.

As I mentioned earlier in this story, Evan Culver got the lion's share of newsprint and got the interviews at the end of the game but he wasted no opportunity to let everyone know who paved the way.

So while everyone talked about Culver, he talked about the Hogs. The guys that blocked for him, Thatcher, Paolini, Harka and others coming out of the backfield. It was just a great, great group of guys.

Evan Culver said the greatest influences in his life were his mom and dad. "Those two set the example and standard for how I want to be and the person I want to be going forward in life." He went on to play football at and graduate from Kutztown University. After a brief nine-year career in the US Army, he's attending flight school while studying to be a helicopter pilot.

Nate Harka briefly attended Kutztown University but stopped playing football due to injuries. He earned a degree in business management with a focus on sports management and currently works in sales at ADP in Allentown, Pennsylvania. He enjoys his job and is successful. Harka emphasizes the coaching style and drills during his middle school years as a key factor shaping his team's success later on.

Christian Carvis liked the camaraderie and discipline of football. "It's one of those sports where you prepare 90% of the time to get on average five seconds per play. But you put hours and hours and hours into the preparation and practice. Days and days and days of preparation for those short little blips of plays. But I also don't know a sport that produces or involves the quantity of good, good men with good character. They lend a great deal of experience to young kids who are extremely malleable and able to soak up good habits, tendencies, little things here and there. I think it played a tremendous part in developing this boy into a man." He played one year at Weidner but left after suffering concussions, hung up the cleats and transferred to West Chester University. Then COVID hit, so he switched majors to communications and wound up taking a job at a finance company.

Ryan Meyers, member of the Hogs, said, "The only low feeling was seeing it all come to an end. I was able to play with some of them in college. But guys like Kane, Paolini, and Thatcher, I'd never get to play with those guys again. So it was a bittersweet moment. Coach Evancho was the best head coach I ever had in high school and growing up. He was a player's coach. One thing that he did, which a lot of other head coaches don't do, is he came out to practice and let his coaches coach. So he would just walk around and throw in a tip here and there. But he never tried to control the practice. And I think that's why the team molded together the way they did. I went to Kutztown, played five years but in four seasons. I can't say enough good things about how lucky we were in high school and then to join a program like Kutztown that was growing. I might have lost fifteen games in high school and college combined. So I am fortunate. At Kutztown, I got to play with Harka, Culver, and Wolfe again.

Meyers also admired the coaching staff. "My greatest influence in high school was Coach Chromczak. From the time I was in eighth grade, I would talk to him and then once I got to high school, he always trusted me. I always took pride in knowing that I had his trust. He definitely cared about turning us into good people and good young men more than winning football games. But in that process we made a damn good football team. I'm definitely able to take criticism. He knew that, so he would test me. From the time I was a freshman, pretty early on I noticed that I was getting tested a little bit more than some other guys. But I just took it as a compliment. He knew me, knew I was going to work hard. I knew he was going to have a game plan ready for us. So I think that was probably the turning point from a young age."

Alstan Wolfe moved to quarterback after his sophomore season and went to Kutztown University after high school to play football. "I played receiver and then ended up quitting after my first year just because it was a heavy load with school and football. I was getting banged up constantly, and my legs were pretty much falling apart. But right after that, I started coaching football with Coach Sams and Coach Chromczak at Southern Lehigh. That's what I've been doing ever since."

Josh Snead, in a further embrace of the coaching staff, said, "One of the things that I really appreciated about the coaches, especially once we got back to practice, was the intensity that they brought every single day. They were also very caring and nurturing. They didn't harp on mistakes; they would come at you about a mistake but then step aside and help you fix it. The intensity was there every single day of practice, which really helped the team out. So they were encouragers. I think when you have that much talent in one place, you have no other choice than to just push them to be great."

Zach Thatcher went to Widener University and graduated at the top of his class in mechanical engineering. Zach continues to achieve, attaining Mechanical Engineer of the Year one year and posting a 3.7 GPA. He made a lot friends. His roommates all played football with him. They all lived in a house together, so it was a gut-wrenching decision to inform those guys that he had decided to walk away from game. He did all the training leading up to the third year. Then about a week or two before the season started, Zach faced the reality that he just couldn't do it. He said, "I don't know if it was because I was playing in the middle of the day. I don't know if it was because I wasn't playing with any of my buddies that I grew up with. My roommate became the quarterback and made all conference. I was best man at his wedding. So I'm really glad that those relationships stuck, because I loved those guys I was playing with in college. But it was not the same as high school. That was very special."

Thatcher reflected on those high school years by saying, "Leading up to our senior year there was this big article that the *Express Times* did about quarterbacks in the Valley. I think there were seven of us. You know, I was labeled something like the traditional QB as a throwback. I think it was the 'throwback' nickname that I got. Because I was really the only one that went in and played offense and defense. Little did anyone know that I hated it."

Mike Kane, remembering his final season at Saucon Valley, said,

"I knew our group of seniors would be something special. We had that bond ever since we were young. To go 14–0 and be the last AAA public school football team left standing in a tournament normally dominated by the prep schools, I didn't envision that happening."

Legendary Sunday's At Coach Chrom's House
Karen Kane added, "Michael was welcomed into the group as an Honorary Hog and allowed to come over and participate occasionally. When he didn't attend, he would always ask, 'what happened?' Christian cooly and calmly cautioned him by saying, 'What happens there stays there,' so to speak, you know, like they didn't talk about things outside of their group there. But Coach Chromczak is a really great guy! He and Michael were very close. They were very close."

There is no doubt that Saucon Football has missed the leadership and hard-nosed efforts of Christian. It is equally obvious that Carvis misses Saucon football as well. Carvis noted that he was most fond of the coaches and atmosphere of the whole program. "Two-a-day practices in particular, because you become so much closer with your teammates." Christian also shared that, "I especially appreciated Coach Chromczak's house every Sunday (for film review and brunch) and wondering what's going to come out of Cody's (Zrinski) mouth next."

Meyers still enjoys talking about game nights.

> We would get out of school and everybody on the offensive line would come to my house. So all the Hogs would come here, and my mom would make them food. We'd eat and try to get our minds off the game. At that point, just try to stay calm. We'd all drive to the stadium together. We go out on the field and warm up and then we come back in to the locker room and have a little meeting with Coach Chromczak, who would draw the plays

we were planning on running on the first drive on the whiteboard. We always scripted the first drive. Then we'd go back in the locker room, and we'd have ten minutes to ourselves, just putting our last little bit of stuff on. Then it would get really quiet, everybody'd be listening to their music, and then Coach [Chrom] would come out. It seemed like every week he blew my mind—one of the best speech givers I know. You'd get hyped up and he'd go back in the office and Coach Evancho would come back out and give us a little bit of a speech. We got down on one knee, prayed, and then went out to the field. Harka was quiet. But everybody knew that he was a leader. Thatcher was quiet. Culver was definitely one of the locker room leaders as far as talking. Carvis would always talk to the whole team or just the offensive line, because he was the only senior on the line. He was definitely the leader of that group that year.

Tougher Regular Season, Easier Playoffs:
As we have seen, Saucon Valley faced tougher opponents during the regular Colonial League season compared to most of the playoff teams. The league might have been top-heavy with a few strong teams at the top and a wider gap between them and the rest. But the stiff Colonial League competition prepared these Panthers to play some tough, perennial playoff teams.

Favorite Games
Coach Sams favors games with high drama, comebacks, and close finishes. The Notre Dame game exemplified this perfectly, showcasing a dramatic shift in momentum and a thrilling conclusion. He says, "From a comfortable lead (35–7) to a nail-biting tie (35–35) at the end, it had everything: a comeback, a game-winning touchdown, and an electric atmosphere." The BECA

game was not his personal favorite, but its significance as the "big game" that propelled them to the playoffs cannot be downplayed. Remembering the Selinsgrove coach commenting, "Good luck against Imhotep," some fans criticized Saucon coaches for keeping Culver in that game. In the end, and despite losing to Imhotep, Sams remembers this game for the competitive spirit and fact they never gave up against the strongest opponent faced all year.

He goes on to say, "By week twelve or thirteen, football season fatigue sets in. The weight room sessions after school became a struggle for the players. We all knew conditioning and weight training were crucial, but the grind was real, and injuries piled up. However, we worried that changing the routine might break our momentum. It felt almost superstitious—we'd been 'doing it this way successfully', so why risk disrupting that rhythm?"

Thanksgiving morning was unique for Sams. "As a varsity coach, it was my only time practicing on the holiday. Except for when I played at Easton High School, I never practiced or played on this day." Easton is a school known for its annual Thanksgiving Day slugfest with New Jersey rival Phillipsburg. The strangeness of this particular morning was enhanced by the amazing spread put on by the parents—bagels, breakfast treats, and ribeye steaks! After practice, he took his son to the Easton-Phillipsburg game, a cherished tradition. "That brought back a flood of memories. The moms surprised everyone with a feast after practice. We all had a good laugh about it!"

Coaching this team was not hard, Sams relates.

> The locker room at halftime, even during those close games like Southern Lehigh, was surprisingly calm. There wasn't any yelling or finger-pointing, just a group of guys focused on playing their best. That season, leadership came from all over the field. We had a strong offensive line led by the experienced Ryan Meyers, along with Steven

Good, Christian Carvis, and Tre Polak. Zach Thatcher, our talented quarterback and free safety, was a true leader by example. Mike Kane and Nate Harka provided quiet leadership through their consistent performance on both offense and defense. We also had a standout versatile player in Mike Paolini who contributed explosively on both sides of the ball. There were many leaders on this team, some vocal, some leading by example, but all united in their love for the game. This positive and focused atmosphere in the locker room is what I remember most about that special season.

The Awards
Anybody that knows Saucon Valley senior football cocaptain Christian Carvis well is aware of his focused intensity and determination. Christian had been playing football that way since he was seven years old. He was all over the field and his tenacious approach was rewarded with All-League, All-Area and All-State honors for the 2015 season.

Not only was Christian recognized for those supreme achievements, but he also became part of the history books at Saucon Valley. The 2015 season saw Christian make eighty-two tackle-assists, bringing his total career assists to 129. Both are still Saucon Valley school records. "My most memorable play of the season was either the hit on Antwon Keenan in the BECA game when Mike Paolini swept his legs out and I finished it, or in the Wilson game when I knocked the kid's helmet off," is what he recalled.

Christian had this piece of advice to anyone playing the game: "Hard work and dedication to the program are most important. Make it about the team and not about yourself. Keep working your [tail] off to make yourself a better football player and it will pay off in the end."

Among Culver's many accolades earned as a Panther were PA

AAA Offensive Player of the Year, *Morning Call* Player of the Year, First Team All-State, All-League, All-Area and 2015 District XI leader in rushing yards (2,934), touchdowns (48), single season total points scored (292) and total career points (470). He finished his Saucon career with 4,937 rushing yards and seventy-seven touchdowns on 536 carries (all school records). He owns ten of the longest runs from scrimmage in school history. Defensively, he ranks second in career interceptions with at least three of those being game-saving grabs. Evan reached the one-thousand-yard rushing club two years in a row.

Nate Harka was a two-time All-League Second Team member and two-time All-Area member with seventeen touchdowns and 1,302 receiving yards for his high school career. He's also second best in career kickoff return yardage with 709.

Mike Kane earned top billing for a career leading twelve sacks at the school, All-League and All-Area teams. On the offensive side of the ball throughout his career, he caught a total of sixteen touchdowns. Mike is also second best in career assisted tackles with ninety-five.

Mike Paolini jumped to the top of the sack leader list right behind Kane, with 10.5 career sacks. Adding his three career interceptions, one for a pick-six, he brought down ball carriers with 128 total tackles in his career.

Josh Snead played soccer and football during his final two years at Saucon Valley. In his first year of football, 2015, he set records that haven't been touched since. He kicked seventy-four extra points, owning both the school's single-season and career kicking records.

Zach Thatcher owns four of the longest runs from scrimmage and is a double member of the one-thousand-yard club (1,883 rushing and 2,549 passing). In 2016 he joined John Killar (1991), Joe Killar (1996) and Chris McKeown (2004) as the winner of the National Football Scholar Athlete Award. For the season, Zach passed for 1,210 yards, scoring fourteen touchdowns, and through his career, he passed for 2,549 yards with thirty-one touchdowns. On the ground he rushed for another 1,164 yards in the season and 1,883 for his career while scoring seventeen touchdowns for the year with a total of twenty-six for his career. Thatcher was totally responsible for having a hand in fifty-seven touchdowns on the ground and through the air.

Alstan Wolfe made THE catch of the year with that leaping grab against Notre Dame!

Bicentennial Cup

Colonial League Champions

District XI Champions

EPILOGUE

It's a game of mistakes. Every play, there are multiple mistakes. So you limit your mistakes. Watching Saucon Valley, one thing you saw is they kept theirs at a minimum.
—Dan Kendra, Allentown Central Catholic quarterbacks coach

GETTING OUTSIDE OF the Colonial League universe of coaches, players, parents, and fans, it's time to hear from a longtime observer of high school football in the Lehigh Valley. Dan Kendra graduated as the all-time leader in passing and total offense at Allentown Central Catholic (ACC) in 1974. As a senior, he made first-team all-state, Prep All-American and was nominated to play in the annual Big 33 game (the thirty-three best high school seniors from Pennsylvania playing the best thirty-three high school players from Ohio). He graduated as the all-time passing and total offense leader at West Virginia University, where he played for legendary coach Bobby Bowden. He played in the NFL for the Los Angeles Rams and had a great coaching career at Bethlehem Catholic, Phillipsburg High School, Nazareth Area High School, and his alma mater, where he added multiple District XI and PIAA State Championships to his resume of accomplishments. So for a man who was an inductee to the McDonald's Lehigh Valley All-Star Football Classic Hall of Fame, engaging in the game for about fifty years mostly at the high school level in the Lehigh Valley to sit with me and talk glowingly about this team—I was honored to hear what he had to say about our 2015 team from Saucon Valley.

Watching them on TV and following them as time allowed, he began to notice Coach Evancho putting together a winning program. ACC played in the East Penn Conference, a big school league where the AAAA schools competed in 2015. Many of these schools are now rated AAAAAA after the PIAA realigned classifications. He noted there's almost an inferiority complex sometimes between leagues and classification levels. One league feels that they're dominant, then a team in another league starts having unparalleled success. How good could that be? One thing that impressed Dan most about this Saucon Valley team was their senior leadership setting the tone. They got into the playoffs a couple of years and were knocked off by what people thought was a superior team (Bethlehem Catholic, also a AAA team from the East Penn Conference). The following year, when they beat Bethlehem Catholic in the District XI play-off game, everybody took notice. That was an eye-opening moment.

Talking about high school football in general, he said, "When teams start to have success, the kids start believing. Once you get sixteen, seventeen, eighteen-year-old kids believing in the program, you've got something special. Somebody once asked a coach before the season started, 'How's the team going to be this year?' The coach said in reply, 'I'll tell you in about ten to fifteen years how good this team was.'"

We're coming up on ten years since this team made their run to the PIAA State Championship, and people still remember them fondly.

Dan went on to say, "High school football can be called the last bastion today of the sport. You're totally dependent on someone else to perform. The game is up front. Those five, six guys tackle to tackle and the tight end, that's the game. Everybody in the stands and watching on the video pays attention to the guy with the ball in his hands. Anybody who's a student of the game knows the game is played up front. The linemen must hit their blocks, make their adjustments and push the guy they're assigned out of the way. It's a game of mistakes. Every play, there are multiple mistakes. So you limit your mistakes. Watching Saucon Valley, one thing you saw is they kept theirs at a minimum."

These linemen, the Hogs, grew up together, learned the game together, bonded with each other, committed to each other, and were probably afraid of letting each other down. They played hard for each other. Dan continued.

> When you see that in kids today—not playing for themselves but playing for each other—you have something special. One great thing about Saucon Valley is that it's a small community. When you have a situation where you don't have the large school environments like Parkland, Liberty, and Easton with huge talent pools to draw from, the feeder system is much more contained, more intimate, limited. A talented group like the 2015 Panthers from a small community makes people sit up and take notice. Next thing you know, the whole community gets involved. There's a self-propelling inertia that takes effect. The adrenalin catches fire outside of the team and expectations continue to rise throughout the season.
>
> Saucon Valley put together a winning season in 2013, then it snowballed in '14. As the 2015 season rolled on, football observers in the Valley started to see something special. Their coaching staff must have done a great job because it's hard to keep kids focused and locked in for that extended period of time—winning fourteen games! Plus back then there were two preseason scrimmages. So you have two scrimmages plus fourteen games. That's an awful big load in a punishing game like football. Then that final game against Imhotep, basically an all-star Philadelphia team, was brutal but not the end of the story. Nobody got by Imhotep that year. They were a constant presence in the state championship for the next few years.

Football is such a game of momentum. You see it swing back and forth in high school football. You think the game is won, then there's an interception, a blocked punt, a lost fumble, costly penalties or a big play, an injured player. In one split-second the energy changes dramatically and your opponent picks up the momentum to shift the game in their favor.

Football teaches you a work ethic. It's very hard. It's kind of funny the way it all pans out but winning and losing does teach character. Dan added,

> Talk to the coaching staff there (at Saucon Valley). This is a common denominator especially in high school football. I'll bet they'll say there's a group of three to four or five kids that have a passion, they want to win so badly. They'll police the rest of the team. You don't have to discipline your team as a coach. Those kids will take care of business themselves. They'll start to see somebody straying off course and correct it, the coach doesn't have to worry about it. A captain or a player on the team will just go like, 'Don't worry coach, I got this.' And they keep their teammates inline. That's a common denominator with successful teams. The kids play the game, and coaches provide the tools.

Saucon Valley had a nucleus of players that created a successful environment in their sophomore and junior years, culminating in their senior year. Here we are ten years later and the stories they tell are far from the wins and losses. They tell you about the kids they remember, something funny that happened, how much fun they had at Coach Chrom's house, the biggest eaters, times hanging out together. It's those kinds of stories that Dan recalled from his own high school days fifty years ago, playing on an undefeated team. Having played at all three levels, he said, "The one thing about high school ball is it's kind of the purest form of the game. They play because they're on that field for pure enjoyment; nobody's getting paid. It's not work. You know, there are no scholarships involved. There's no money involved. You're there because you have a passion to play the game. I have fifty-year friends from my high school team. We stay in touch. If they're in the area, we see each other. If they're outside the area, we stay in touch. When you say goodbye, the last thing you say to him is, 'I love you, man.'" That's what these guys have in common with each other.

As the 2015 season progressed, the feeling across the whole Lehigh Valley was, 'Who are these guys?' But then as you saw them play, personnel wise, you noticed they had a very good bunch of athletes. It wasn't just your average high school team. They had some solid competition in Notre Dame, Southern Lehigh, and Northwestern Lehigh. Saucon Valley had more capable athletes across the board. Their quarterback, running back, receivers, Hogs, and secondary held a number of different players that could have played at Parkland (who went on to play in the AAAA State Championship Game) or any other team. They could have played anywhere across the Lehigh Valley and been great players. It wasn't just that they were great players at Saucon Valley. They had a passion that oozed out and as an opposing player when you saw them coming, you knew they meant business.

It's the team that runs, blocks, and tackles. A team that runs well as a group, tackles, and blocks is a team that wins. Everybody watches the football because that's just what people are drawn to; the guy with the ball in his hands, the thrower, the receiver. But everything happening around them is the more vital part of the game. That offensive line is the most valuable commodity on the football field, by far. Things change and on every play from scrimmage those offensive linemen are constantly making adjustments, calling out assignments, changing blocking techniques. What's going to happen when you get to the next level from the line, you have to handle the linebackers. Okay, get up to the second level on that linebacker, or cornerback. If your center is good enough that he can kick, pull in and wrap on a linebacker, it's miraculous.

Another thing about high school football that's unique is when you get a high school kid who's a freshman or sophomore and watch their development. Some have raw talent; some have to grow into their skills. Kids come in as ninth graders, thirteen- to fourteen-year-old kids. They're still boys, and then over the next two to three years, you watch them mature into young men. You'll see that growth spurt, maturity develops, they'll stronger, skills will blossom, and confidence will grow.

The kids sense when coaching staffs really gel together. They feed off it, as we've seen.

The bottom line on this 2015 Panther team that Dan Kendra wanted the coaches and the kids to know is that coaches and other players in the Lehigh Valley—whether they want to admit it or not—were impressed and proud of them. That's the one thing he says he likes about coaching in this area. "It doesn't matter what team it is. If a team advances in the state playoffs he says, "I'm all for them. I want them to excel. Again, like I said, I am proud of a local team, especially from a small community like the Saucon Valley School District, excelling like they did."

ACKNOWLEDGMENTS

WRITING A BOOK is a marathon, not a sprint, and during this marathon, I tripped several times, nearly face-planting on a few of those. Thankfully, these wonderful people were there to catch me. Everyone listed here. The team, coaches, parents, reporters, and Hellertown and Lower Saucon Township residents and businesses listened and told me the stories of these grown men who had started out as 80-pounders. All the teams who competed and pushed these guys to become who they are today made this story.

Throughout my eight years of recording statistics for this team, Duke Helm kept me honest with his phenomenal statistical recording of all District XI stats. He covered more than forty schools. I only had one to worry about, so I feel his pain of striving for accuracy and I'm thankful that I could still go back and look at his record keeping to provide an accurate accounting.

I want to apologize for not interviewing everyone I would have liked to meet for this story. Time, distance, and logistics simply wouldn't allow it. I had reached out to numerous people associated with this team who never responded to me. Others were very gracious with their time and comments, and I'm grateful to have this opportunity to capture the 2015 Saucon Valley Football story for posterity.

What follows is some praise for people who have helped me along the way.

First, I'm thankful to my Lord and Savior Jesus Christ for granting me the ability to interview people, write and edit a story, and put this whole process in motion. Without Him, I would be nothing. With Him, I've been able to craft this glowing account of a time in our lives that was exciting, gratifying, and at times dream-like—but always hopeful.

I owe a tremendous debt of gratitude to my high school English teacher, Oleva Lewis, who also served as the publisher of the Neosho County Community Junior College newspaper. She recognized my potential as a writer early on, taking a chance and appointing me as the first freshman newspaper editor of that school. Her dedication to her craft and her patience with a novice like me laid the foundation for my writing skills. I would be lost for words today if it weren't for her mentorship.

David Smale, my friend, mentor, and fellow writer (though with significantly more published works!) has been my guiding light since editing my first novel, *Honor Through Sacrifice*.

Bob Frey has been my partner in developing this story. As the athletic director during these historic seasons, he agreed to sponsor this work, has connected me with players and coaches, helped with the backstory content, and has patiently awaited this day.

Keith Riefenstahl is a sports reporter for the *Saucon Source* who provided pregame, in-game, and postgame insight for each game. Much of the commentary in this book was originally written by Keith. He and his publisher, Josh Popichak, have graciously authorized me to use it here.

Tom Housenick is a sports reporter at *The Morning Call*. Thank you for writing the kind Foreword to this story and granting me the release to use some of your postgame article content.

Matt Evancho, head football coach, opened up his personal story to share with us all. I first met Coach when my youngest son started playing on his JV team as a freshman years ago. That's when I volunteered to keep stats for his team. He was a rock then and he remains so today. He still keeps in touch with his coaches.

Phil Sams, receiver's coach, was my son's coach. Phil is a friendly man and has a magnetic personality that everyone loves. Phil has always been kind and helpful, providing keen insight into this team. He keeps in touch with his players.

Ed Chromczak was the offensive coordinator who kept that Saucon Valley train running. He has provided great insight into the Hogs. He loves these guys and it's obvious they love him. He held a skull session every Sunday after a game with his line at his home, to cover the learning opportunities his players need to own and digest. He still has photos and newspaper clippings of their games on his wall at home and keeps in touch with his players.

Chris Labatch, Saucon Valley defensive coordinator, provided great insight into the backstory and his long-standing friendship with Matt Evancho. He led that lock-down defense throughout the year. He also keeps in touch with his players.

Zach Thatcher has been a great point of contact for me, connecting me with many of the players that I've interviewed and quoted in this story.

Gail Nolf, friend and game-day announcer, was gracious and friendly in the press box at Montford Illick Stadium. He loves football and more importantly he loves these players. He also keeps in touch with them.

The 2006–2015 Panther football team members: thank you for giving me a reason to write this book and giving us all an exciting football team to watch, support, and ride alongside.

The parents, Vickie Wolfe, Karen and Paul Kane, Barb and Jim Thatcher, Brenda Carvis, Joleyce Adams, Kim Kemmerer: thank you for sharing your stories and pictures.

Dan Kendra is well-known in and around Lehigh Valley football circles. His independent take on this team in their glory days draws a parallel to his own glory days fifty years ago. He provided captivating observations.

Brad Wilson, sports reporter for *Lehigh Valley Live*, helped with stories he wrote a decade ago, not knowing they would end up in this book. He has given me authorization to use his content.

My thanks also go to John Koehler and his exceptional publishing team (Becky Hilliker and Danielle Koehler) at Köehler Books. His team guides me, corrects me, puts up with me, and has been with me from the beginning. He overlooks some of my quirks, giving me the benefit of the doubt in certain cases and keeping me grounded in others with this, my third book.

And a thank you to Rae Lynn Vittorino, who believes in me and graciously agreed to proofread this manuscript as my beta reviewer. She's been great, always has a wonderful personality, and is a sister for whom I would push through a brick wall.

The journey to this book began with a whisper, an idea that needed fertile ground to grow. I'm grateful to everyone who provided the sunshine and nourishment.

Lastly, the Saucon Valley School Community offered this grateful poem, and I report it here out of gratitude and appreciation for the best year of our lives:

Thank You, Panthers, For A Great Season!
Hail the Panther football team, the mighty Red and Black!
The worthiest of warriors, the leaders of the pack.
This season's been one for the books—a truly awesome ride,
In which we all of Saucon Valley take the highest pride.
You started out the season winning, but still underrated,
Which made your triumphs in the playoffs most appreciated.
You demonstrated just how poise, hard work, and discipline
Yield a team that's tough, fights hard, and finds a way to win.
The League and District crowns were yours, then, in the playoffs, you

Defeated BECA handily, and then Lehighton, too.
You carried on your winning ways by beating Scranton Prep,
And did the same to Selinsgrove, who had a fearsome rep.
Imhotep was big and quick, and, yes, they won the game,
But you won respect and admiration, just the same.
You battled them and battled them, through sheer determination.
You more than earned the convoy home, with sirens' celebration.
Let's salute you men of heart and class and spirit, too:
Curtis, Garrett, Alstan, Brandon, Connor, Kory, Drew,
Cody, Andrew, Tyler, Tanner, Adam, Dino, Evan,
TJ, RJ, Gavin, Chris, Kyle, Jared, Devan.
Two Nates, three Zachs, two Ryans, two Justins, Tim, Brentt, Abe, and Hayden,
Two Patricks, Josh, two Mikes, two Christians, Trey, Cole, Shaun, and Braden.
We've only got a few more of the gallant crew to go:
Steven, Stephen, Riley, then just Joe and Angelo.
Assistants Chromczak, two Labatches, Sams, and Riefenstahl,
Lenehan, and Kemmerer all went beyond the call.
But we know the lion's share of credit ought to go
To the man who made it work—Head Coach Matt Evancho.
To Every Member of the Saucon Valley Football Team,
We're Proud of You.
The Saucon Valley School Community,
December 14, 2015

REFERENCES

LehighValleyLive.com—Lehighvalleylive.com is owned by Advance Publications. Some of the sports stories written by Brad Wilson, Josh Folck, and Greg Joyce are referenced in this manuscript and used with authorization. Lehighvalleylive.com is the website for *The Express-Times*, a daily newspaper based in Easton, Pennsylvania.

Saucon Source—*Saucon Source* is owned by Josh Popichak, a veteran local journalist, owner, publisher, and editor. Many of the game day stories written by Keith Riefenstahl for this publication have been used with permission.

The Morning Call—*The Morning Call*, formerly owned by Tribune Publishing, is now owned by Alden Global Capital, a New York City-based hedge fund. Senior Reporter Tom Housenick's stories are referenced here with permission. He also wrote the Foreword.

APPENDIX A

TEAM PHOTO

Team Photo, Photo credit: Brenda Carvis

APPENDIX B

DAY IN THE LIFE OF A FOOTBALL PROGRAM

Do you ever wonder what the week of preparation for a football game includes? You might be interested in what the Panthers went through in practice every week during their high school playing careers. Thanks to Head Coach Matt Evancho, here is a look at their practice schedules.

Saturday
- Rest from previous night's game for the players
- Coaches review previous game highs and lows; study film of upcoming opponent

Sunday
- Coaches review the previous game with players, pointing out critiques of what they did well and not so well
- Players get into light practice, to keep loose (warm-up and stretch, address injuries and muscle soreness with the trainer)

Monday/Tuesday
- Coaches continue to develop game plan for upcoming game
- JV players and coaches prep for and attend Monday night JV game
- Players get back into routines (warm-up, stretch, conditioning/fitness period, weight lifting exercises, drills by skillset, pads, address injuries and muscle soreness with the trainer)

Wednesday
2:30–3:00—JV lift, varsity study hall
3:35–3:45—Offensive walk-through to install the Imhotep game plan
3:45–3:55—Warm-up and stretch
3:55–4:15—Defensive Combo/7-on-7
(Focus is on seeing and reacting to opponent's run and pass plays.)
4:15–4:28—Water break and Team Defense
(11-on-11 period where the Panther scout team will show opponent's offense at full speed against the Panther starting defense.)
4:28–4:35—Special Teams: Punt Team
4:35–4:55—Offensive Combo/7-on-7
(Focus on running select offensive runs and passes against opponent's defense.)
4:55–5:02—Special Teams: Kickoff Return Team
5:02–5:20—Water break and Team Offense
(11-on-11 period where the Panthers run their offense full speed against the scout team's interpretation of opponent's defense.)
5:20–5:25—Special Teams: Extra Point/Field Goal
5:25–5:30—"Dessert:" Sprints
(Conditioning/fitness period.)
5:30–5:35—Team Stretch
5:35–5:40—Post-practice position meetings

Thursday
2:30–3:00—Varsity lift, JV study hall
3:35–3:45—Defensive walk-through to install the upcoming game plan
3:45–3:55—Warm-up and stretch
3:55–4:00—Special Teams: Kickoff Team

4:00–4:10—Tackling Stations with four groups
    (emphasis on "open field" tackling)
4:10–4:20—Defensive Groups
    (Defensive Line, linebackers, and defensive backs breakout with their position coaches, refining their skills and techniques.)
4:20–4:38—Water break and Team Defense
    (Includes "Red Zone" defense)
4:38–4:45—Special Teams: Punt Return Team
4:45–4:55—Offensive Groups
    (Hogs, quarterbacks, running backs and receivers break out with their position coaches and refine their skills and try to perfect technique.)
4:55–5:05—Option Period
    (Running the option takes a lot of practice and the Panthers hit hard here.)
5:05–5:25—Water break and Team Offense
    (The last five minutes is dedicated to "Red Zone" offense.)
5:25–5:40 "Dessert," Team Stretch and post practice position meetings

- Players prepare all their gear for the next day's game; if it's away, they pack their bags for the road trip

Friday
- Gameday (rest before game; arrive at stadium at designated time; get on bus at designated time if it's a road trip)
- Pregame prep (dress, see trainer and equipment manager for last minute adjustments)

7:00—Game Time

APPENDIX C

PIAA, DISTRICT XI & COLONIAL LEAGUE

The Saucon Valley School District (SVSD) is a small suburban public school district located in Northampton County, Pennsylvania in the Lehigh Valley region of eastern Pennsylvania. Serving the borough of Hellertown and Lower Saucon Township, the SVSD encompasses approximately 20 square miles bordering Bucks County.

For competitive school sports, SVSD is a member of both the Colonial League and District XI of the PIAA (Pennsylvania Interscholastic Athletic Association).

The PIAA is a non-profit, voluntary membership corporation. The members of PIAA consist of almost all of the public junior high/middle and senior high schools, some of the charter and private junior high/middle schools, and many of the charter and private senior high schools in the Commonwealth of Pennsylvania. Generally stated, the function of PIAA is to develop and enforce rules regulating interscholastic athletic competition, which are authorized or adopted by the member schools.

PIAA was formed in Pittsburgh on December 29, 1913, by a group of high school Principals who wanted to eliminate abuses, establish uniform rules, and place interscholastic athletics in the overall context of secondary education. The purposes of PIAA, as set forth in ARTICLE II of its Constitution, are to:

- Organize, develop, and direct an interscholastic athletic program which will promote, protect, and conserve the health and physical welfare of all participants.
- Formulate and maintain policies that will safeguard the educational values of interscholastic athletics and cultivate the high ideals of good sportsmanship.
- Promote uniformity of standards in all interscholastic athletic competition.

According to their website (www.piaa.org) PIAA membership consists of 1,431 schools, of which 583 are senior high schools and 594 are junior high/middle schools. Of that membership, 40 are charter senior high schools, 144 are private senior high schools, 17 are charter junior high/middle schools, and 53 are private junior high/middle Schools. More than 350,000 students participate in interscholastic athletics at all levels (varsity, junior varsity, or otherwise) of competition under PIAA jurisdiction, which places Pennsylvania sixth highest among the states for the 2017-2018 scholastic year. Similar associations exist in all 50 states.

PIAA is divided for administrative purposes into 12 geographic districts, each of which has a district committee elected by the member schools within the PIAA district. SVSD is a member of District XI and within that district, they are members of the Colonial League.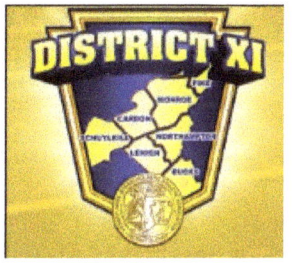

The Colonial League provides championships in a total of 17 sports over all 3 sports seasons, and encompasses the east-central portion of Pennsylvania, including the counties of Carbon, Lehigh, Monroe, Northampton and Schuylkill. Thirteen schools are members and in football, each team schedules nine other teams, rotating in off-

years so that eventually, every school plays each other.

Champions and some additional qualifiers advance to the PIAA Playoffs, culminating in the ultimate goal of a PIAA State Championship.

First, in order to advance to the State Tournament, a team must win their league championship, and then win playoff games at their district level. Beyond that, regional competition matching districts against each other offers a single-elimination tournament bracket with a clear roadmap to the State PIAA Tournament, where the finals are held every year in Hershey, Pennsylvania.

The Schuylkill / Colonial League Football Scheduling Cooperative formed after January of 2019 will not be addressed here, although some Schuylkill teams will be mentioned in the playoff stories that come up later in this book as they provided opposition to Saucon Valley during the Panthers' march through the State Tournament.

APPENDIX D

PHOTO GALLERY

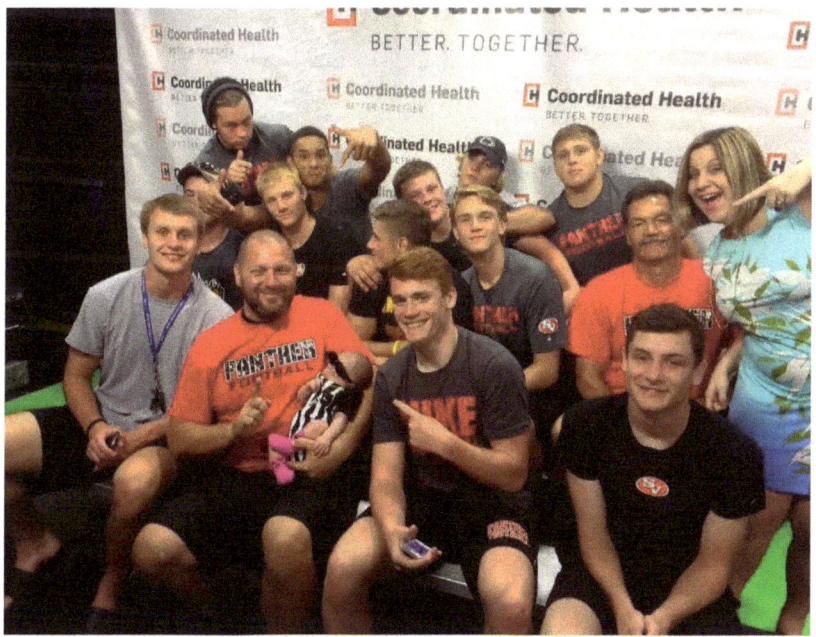

Photos by Kerry Kemmerer

Photo by Vickie Wolfe

Photo by Bob Frey

Photo by Bob Frey

Photo by Karen Kane

Photos by Laura Zaharakis

2015 High School Football Roster

#1 – Josh Snead	#23 – Zach Petiet	#60 – Tim Weaver
#2 – Brentt Bauer	#25 – Garrett Hudak	#61 – Devan VanVliet
#3 – Evan Culver	#27 – Justin Kyra	#62 – Zach Meyers
#4 – Kory Kemmerer	#30 – Dino Zaharakis	#63 – Tyler Miller
#5 – Alstan Wolfe	#32 – Nate Kehs	#64 – Jared Harka
#6 – Connor Jucewicz	#33 – Christian Alling	#65 – Stephen Good
#7 – Zach Thatcher	#34 – Steven Rose	#66 – Hayden Clifford
#8 – Patrick Beatty	#43 – Abe Lugo	#70 – Cole Schreck
#9 – Chris Smith	#44 – Angelo Mahaffey	#71 – Justin Nival
#11 – Joe Naiburg	#48 – Mike Paolini	#72 – Andrew Kline
#12 – Brandon Holub	#49 – Curtis Clifford	#74 – Ryan Meyers
#13 – Ryan Holub	#50 – TJ Rukambe	#75 – Trey Polak
#14 – Gavin Medei	#51 – RJ Massey	#76 – Cody Zrinski
#18 – Riley Haggerty	#52 – Shaun Reily	#80 – Patrick Morrissey
#20 – Tanner Morgan	#53 – Christian Carvis	#81 – Drew Wagner
#21 – Nate Harka	#56 – Braden Hudak	#82 – Mike Kane
#22 – Adam Hough	#58 – Kyle Malone	

Head Coach – Matt Evancho **Trainer** – Amy Virden

Assistant Coaches –
 Ed Chromczak   Eddie Labatch
 Chris Labatch   David Lenehan
 Phil Sams

Team Physicians –
 Dr. David Skillinge
 Dr. Christopher Hawkins

Equipment Manager – Kerry Kemmerer   **Statistician** – Robert Lofthouse

Manager – Ty Kessler   **Water Boy** – Kyle Evancho

Photo by Kim Kemmerer

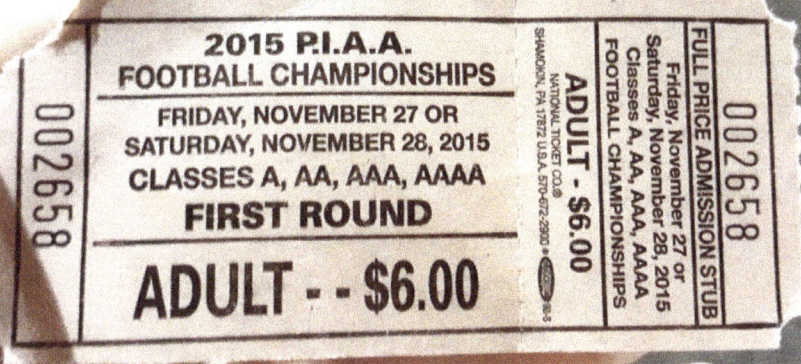

Photo by Saucon Source

Photo by Bob Frey

Photo by Paul Kane

www.ingramcontent.com/pod-product-compliance
Lightning Source LLC
LaVergne TN
LVHW051040070526
838201LV00067B/4875